AMERICA
OFF-LINE

THE COMPLETE OUTERNET STARTER KIT

BY A. J. JACOBS

CADER BOOKS
NEW YORK

ANDREWS AND MCMEEL
A Universal Press Syndicate Company
Kansas City

New to Reality? Not quite ready for this "book" thing? Then take a look at our web site at http://www.caderbooks.com and ease yourself into it.

Thank you for buying this Cader Book—we hope you enjoy it. And thanks as well to the store that sold you this, and the hardworking rep who sold it to them. It takes a lot of people to make a book. Here are some of the many who were instrumental:

EDITORIAL:
Camille N. Cline, Jake Morrissey, Dorothy O'Brien, Regan Brown

DESIGN:
Charles Kreloff

COPY EDITING/PROOFING:
Miranda Ottewell, Bill Bryan, Dan Kulkosky

PRODUCTION:
Carol Coe, Cathy Kirkland

LEGAL:
Renee Schwartz, Esq.

If you would like to share any thoughts about this book, or are interested in other books by us, please write to Cader Books, 38 E. 29 Street, New York, NY 10016.

Library of Congress Cataloging-in-Publication Data
Jacobs, A.J., 1968-
    America off-line / by A.J. Jacobs. — 1st ed.
        p. cm.
    ISBN 0-8362-2433-7 (pbk.)
    1. Electronic data processing—Humor. 2. Reality—Humor.
I. Title.
PN6231.E4J33 1996   96-32362
818'.5407—dc20   CIP

FIRST EDITION
10 9 8 7 6 5 4 3 2 1

ATTENTION SCHOOLS AND BUSINESSES
Andrews and McMeel books are available at quantity discounts with bulk purchase for educational, business, or sales promotional use. For information, please write to: Special Sales Department, Andrews and McMeel, 4520 Main Street, Kansas City, Missouri 64111.

TABLE OF
CONTENTS

ACKNOWLEDGMENTS

Multiple thanks to my family,
Susan Dominus, Camille Cline, Michael Cader,
my intelligent agent Sloan Harris,
and my trusty No. 2 Eberhard Faber

THE SIGN-OFF

Dear Potential Member:

Take a moment and imagine this: You get up in the morning. You check the stock market. You dash off a letter to your Uncle Merv. You go shopping for new snow tires. You "meet" some friends and gab about last night's *X-Files* episode.

Now here's the amazing part: You do all these things WITHOUT the help of your computer. That's right—completely off-line. No keyboard, no mouse, no screeching modem!

Sound like something out of rec.arts.tv.twilight-zone? It's not. It's here today, it's reasonably priced and it's called...America Off-Line.

What Is America Off-Line?

America Off-Line is the revolutionary service that links you to an eye-popping interactive world known as "nonvirtual Reality"—or, more simply, "Reality." Enter this world (located just outside your computer!) and you may never want to leave. Just look at what you'll have access to:

•**A friendly community.** America Off-Line boasts a

jaw-dropping 250 million members; that's more visitors than the *Beavis and Butt-head* Web site got all last year! You'll love interacting with fellow users in our famous chat rooms (or "parties").

•**A sea of information.** Join up, and you'll be swimming in more data than can be contained in a dozen hard drives! We've got thousands of newspapers and magazines, dozens of nonelectronic "libraries," and unlimited "mail" delivered to your door every day but Sunday by a real human being.

•**Convenience.** Talk about easy access! Our system, available 24 hours, is compatible with all Macintosh, PC, and UNIX platforms. Plus you'll enjoy powerful multitasking capabilities: Ride your exercise bike, talk on the phone, and watch *Rhoda,* all at the same time!

•**Superior graphics and sound.** Reality boasts a full-color palette with *millions* of hues and an astounding pixel density. (If you want even more clarity, you can upgrade with glasses or contacts.) You'll enjoy full-motion visuals that make QuickTime look neolithic, and acoustics to rival SoundBlaster. *Special bonus:* With America Off-Line, you never have to wait for free art to download. Simply go to one of America Off-Line's Museum sites!

•**High transmission speed.** The default speed for Reality is a breakneck 60 seconds per minute. That's pretty darn fast, and should be enough for most of our members. Still, there will always be those Antsy Andrews who want even more, which is why we provide accelerators. Buy them at Starbucks or, if you prefer the powder version, at the bathroom of select nightclubs.

•**The Outernet.** With America Off-Line, you'll gain access to an even vaster network known as the Outernet, which encompasses the popular World Wide World. Current membership: 5 billion and growing!

Sound enticing? We think so too. That's why we made it so easy for you to sign off. Here's what you need:

Memory Requirements

The only memory necessary to run America Off-Line is that contained in your cranium. It features both RAM (the name of the sushi bar where you're meeting your mother tonight) and ROM (the name of your mother).

Softwear Requirements

To navigate Reality, you'll need some basic softwear, or "clothes," as they're called off-line. In addition to the Fruit of the Looms that have served all your needs up till now, you'll also need pants, shirts, skirts, blouses, ties, bras and cummerbunds, depending on whether your operating system is male or female. Bundled softwear (aka "suits") is also available.

Local Access Requirements

America Off-Line can be accessed from anywhere in the United States. And we mean anywhere: the Mojave Desert, your bathroom, wherever. And since there's no access number to dial, it's rarely busy.

Disconnecting

When you're ready to pull onto the Information Driveway, just follow these easy steps:

1. Click to the Exit option on your on-line service.

2. Press the Off button on your terminal. (This is often located in the back. You might have to actually lift your butt off the chair to find it.)

3. Unplug your computer.

4. (optional) Stick your computer in the back of your closet next to the yogurt maker used twice in 1983.

And that's it. You're officially off-line. That wasn't so bad, eh? Troubleshooting Tip: If that method did not work, try rebooting your computer and hitting your monitor with a large slab of limestone.

Estimated disconnect time: One second.

The Starter Screen

Once you have signed off, you'll look up from your monitor and see the Starter Screen, also called "your room." No doubt you'll be impressed by America Off-Line's colorful graphic interface. Talk about what-you-see-is-what-you-get (WYSIWYG); objects not only look like what they are, they actually *are* what they are!

Your Starter Screen features many flashy, customized icons. There's the People Connection icon, known off-line as your "spouse." (This icon will give you the special America Off-Line greeting: "It's about goddamn time you looked up from the keyboard.") There's the News icon (you will recognize this by the pile of unread newspapers in the corner), and there's the Desktop icon (the wooden thing underneath all those software packages).

We'll get to all these in due time. Right now, you should keep downloading. Or, as they say off-line, read on!

Operating Your Starter Kit

The rectangular object you are holding in your hands is called a "book" (pronounced like "Power-book," but faster to say). The "book" is essentially a very long text file, but if you've gotten this far, you've probably noticed something strange: There's no scroll bar, no hypertext links, not even a Continue button. No, to navigate the book, you must actually grasp the upper right-hand corner of each "page" and turn right to left. Try it—but come back! Good. Later on, if you get tired and want to keep your place, just use an off-line "bookmark." These handy tools are similar to the ones on the World Wide Web—except that they always fall out.

A. J. JACOBS
Director of Services
America Off-Line

USER NAMES

No doubt you're pretty accustomed to your cyberhandle, whether it be DeathStar99, PezLover, or what have you. After all, that's what you've been called for as long as you can remember. Well, get ready for some fun! Part of the adventure of joining our service is getting your own unique America Off-Line User Name.

But whoa there, pardner. Before you settle on an off-line User Name, you've got to understand that they look and sound somewhat different from on-line handles. In fact, they may seem downright strange at first. But if you want to look cool out there in Reality, you've got to try fitting in. Here's a handy guide to choosing a name.

Rule: Your User Name should contain NO NUMBERS.
Exceptions: "Three" is acceptable in certain areas of Connecticut, as in Chester Taftwood III. "Four" is also okay, but steer clear of Chester Taftwood69.

Rule: Select a nice mix of consonants and vowels. FWxrp may look cool on-line, but it's hard to say at a cocktail party.
Exceptions: New York City taxicab drivers.

Rule: Avoid references to science fiction. Tracy is okay. TribbleTzar is not. Xavier is good. X-Phile is not.
Exceptions: None.

Rule: Adopt TWO names. Most members have both a first name (as in Jill) and a second name (as in Johnson).
Exceptions: A single name is acceptable if you are either a famous movie star (e.g., Cher), a model (e.g., Amber) or a biblical figure (e.g., Moses).

Rule: Do not spell your name phonetically. The name Luke is not spelled "Lewk." The name Jones is not spelled "Jonez."
Exceptions: Rap stars.

Rule: The first letter of each of your names should be capitalized; all others should be lowercase.
Exceptions: Exceedingly pretentious people and/or poets.

Rule: Your name should contain no references to your anatomical features. TenInchTommy, for instance, is no good.
Exceptions: Guys named "Red."

Rule: Keep military titles to a minimum. Captain Sarcastic and Admiral Smurf would be unwelcome in Reality.
Exceptions: You are actually *in* the military.

Rule: Avoid references to science fiction.
(Just making sure you got that one.)

Once you've chosen your User Name, commit it to memory. (You may want to write it down in a safe place.) You'll need to know it. You see, when you interact on America Off-Line, your User Name is not always displayed simultaneously. All right, *sometimes* it is. For instance, if you're on a bowling team or if you've paid $500 to attend a banquet with vulcanized chicken and eye-glazing speeches that last longer than a Kurosawa movie, chances are your User Name is in full view on your chest. But these are exceptions. Generally, when you interface with other America Off-Line members, you're going to have to vocally inform them of your User Name. This is called "introducing yourself." Here's how you do it:

"Hello, I'm (User Name)."
Or, if you're in sales, "(User Name). Damn glad to meet you!"

Eventually, you'll get so used to vocalizing your User Name, you won't think twice about it. But before you get too comfortable, consider this: You're expected to remember *other* people's User Names as well. Sound impossible? Sometimes it is. That's why America Off-Line has words like "dude," "sport," and "fella." Here's how this works:

Other Person: "Hey, John!"
John: "Hey, dude!"
OP: "How ya doin', John?"
John: "Fine, sport. How about you?"
OP: "Great. How's your wife, Ellen?"
John: "Good, thanks. And how about, um, Mrs. dude?"
(A third person enters the conversation.)
Third Person: "Hello there, John!"
John: "Hey, fella!...Fella, do you know dude?"

Here are a couple FAQs, or "frequently asked questions," as we call them on America Off-Line.

Q: *Are some User Names better than others?*
A: Good question. Although it's hard to say what's

better and what's worse, some User Names do give you more freedom—allowing you to access a wider variety of sites. What do we mean? Well, to use an analogy from the on-line world, if your name is Buttmunch44, you might not be welcome in the Kantian Metaphysics Forum. Similarly, on America Off-Line, if your last name ends with *inski* or *stein*, the folks at the Greenwich Yacht and Plaid Pants Club might not invite you in.

Q: *If I don't like my User Name, can I change it?*
A: Yes, you can. But be reasonable. For instance, one Minneapolis-based member changed his name to an unpronounceable symbol that looks like some stray marks on a fourth-grader's notebook. For most people, this would have caused us to revoke their service. This member, however, has bodyguards.

Q: *Can I have multiple pseudonyms, like I do on-line?*
A: Again, the answer is yes. But be warned, pseudonyms are mostly associated with unpleasant people— for instance, murderers wanted by the FBI or overly cute couples. (In the former case, pseudonyms include Bruno the Weasel, The Fixer, and Three-Finger Willy. In the latter case, pseudonyms include Shnookie, Sweetums, and Three-Finger Willy.)

Q: *What about an Anonymous function?*
A: This too is quite rare off-line, unless you're writing something really, really naughty, like a dirty limerick on the bathroom wall, or a roman à clef about the president's inner circle.

THE DESKTOP

Whether you want to write the Great American Novel, fill out a spreadsheet or scribble threatening messages to your ex-fiancé—America Off-Line is the service for you! Our desktop tools are, bar none, the most powerful in the business.

The Word Processor

Perhaps no piece of hardware is more important than the official America Off-Line Word Processor, also known as a "pencil." (Say PEN-sill.) Many of our members think it's more user-friendly than Microsoft Word and Lotus combined! After a while, you'll wonder how you managed without it. Consider these features:

• **Sleek, ergonomic design.** Not only does the "pencil" look attractive, but thanks to the latest microtechnology, it's extremely compact. In fact, so small is the pencil, it makes your laptop look like HAL 9000 on steroids! Even the Newton is a big ugly hulking thing by comparison. The ultraportable pencil slides neatly behind your ear, or even into your front shirt pocket, if you don't mind looking like a luzer.

• **Sophisticated text formatting.** The pencil offers easy-to-master page numbering, footnotes, and borders. And with its advanced design capability, you can even spice up your presentation with customized graphics, or "doodles."

• **An automatic Save function.** Every letter, word, sentence and paragraph is saved immediately, as soon as it is entered onto the "paper." (Paper is similar to your computer screen, except it lies flat and won't emit rays that give your unborn child six elbows.)

Purchasing Your Word Processor

You'll probably want to buy your Word Processor at an authorized dealer such as Staples or Sears. And here's some good news: Unlike your computer, your America Off-Line Word Processor won't become obsolete as you carry it home from the store. In fact, in the last several decades, the basic operating system hasn't changed very much at all.

That helps keep costs way down. With a little comparison shopping, you can find a "pencil" for less than half the price of the Hewlett-Packard Vectra XU. Or about US$0.10.

But don't be too much of a skinflint! Stick to the major platforms: either Eberhard Faber or Mongol, both of which offer versions 1.0, 2.0, and 3.0. (Unless you need to fill out little ovals on a standardized test, one version is as good as another.)

One caution: "Pencils" have built-in limits to the number of words they can process. In on-line terms, figure on approximately 50 rants about the Power Rangers' spandex uniforms and the embarrassing

The Parts

Operation

Although America Off-Line does offer classes in how to operate the Word Processor (see "Education" in "Kids' Stuff," page 63), most of our members can master this dynamic tool themselves. Just follow these directions:

1. Hold the "pencil" upright between your thumb and forefinger. (Important: Do not squeeze too hard, or you might get the off-line version of carpal tunnel syndrome, known as "writer's cramp.")

2. Lower the "pencil" onto a piece of paper and emulate the shapes that are on your keyboard.

3. If you make a mistake, edit your document with the powerful Delete function: Simply turn the "pencil" upside down, thus activating the "eraser." (*Special bonus:* The eraser is a lot more fun to chew than your keyboard.)

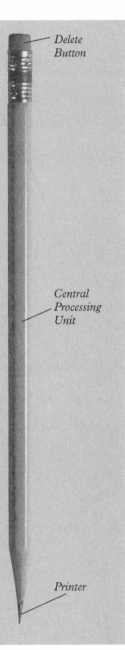

Delete Button

Central Processing Unit

Printer

*Word Processor
repair kit*

bulges they reveal. That's about all one pencil can handle. Then it burns out.

In the meantime, you'll need to give your "pencil" the occasional tune-up. Do-it-yourselfers can buy the repair kit, called the "pencil sharpener." Or you can take your pencil to the dealer and tell them something's wrong. They'll be happy to help you out, after placing a discreet call to the sanatorium.

Maintenance

Keep your pencil at room temperature and in a dry place. You might want to buy the special America Off-Line Word Processor Carrying Case, called a "mug."

HOT TIP: After you've created a document with your "pencil," be sure to back it up and save it to another folder. Otherwise, something might go wrong and your precious words might get garbled. Everyone has a horror story about this. For instance, a system called The Dog always seems to be eating files, especially geometry homework. You'll feel much safer if you back it up with one of America Off-Line's Save options, which include "carbon copies" and "Xerox."

Beyond the Pencil

As you start using your America Off-Line Word Processor more and more, you may find yourself hungering for other powerful desktop tools. Luckily, we provide a wide range of cutting-edge upgrades and additions, all developed within the last millennium.

FILE COMPRESSOR

This device—also known as a "rubber band"—takes your files and squeezes them so they take up much less space on your desktop. To unstuff, remove digitally—i.e., with the fingers. (Note: File Compressors double as a fun game for kids, who shoot them at their friends. The game is similar to Mortal Kombat, except none of the players gets his heart ripped out and stuck on a pole.)

Multiple-license network version of our File Compressor

FILE ATTACHING FUNCTION

Unlike on-line, this function is purchased separately in Reality. Members can choose between two pieces of hardware: the "paper clip" and the "stapler." Both are compatible with all types of files, though the stapler is more permanent.

Basic and power user File Attachers

CUT-AND-PASTE FUNCTION

The pencil's built-in editor is pretty darn powerful, but if you want another option, you can buy this Word Processor upgrade, also known as "scissors and tape." Still, be warned: cutting and pasting isn't as popular with America Off-Line documents as it is on-line. Unless you are writing a document that says "WE HAVE YOUR TOMMY— DO NOT CALL THE POLICE," try to keep cutting and pasting to a minimum.

One cuts, one pastes

HIGHLIGHTED TEXT FUNCTION

This is used most often in chemistry and Latin text-books. You may be confused at first: no matter how many times you press highlighted text, it won't link you to another site. Its biggest advantage is that it looks cooler than underlining.

ADDITIONAL STORAGE

Your desktop provides an impressive amount of storage—about the equivalent of 125 megabytes. Still, for those advanced users who want even more capacity, there are several upgrades available. The File Cabinet offers about 250 megs with the easy access of a Zip drive. The Closet offers between 500 and 700 megs, depending on the size of your sneaker collection. And the Basement offers 3 gigabytes, though good luck ever finding anything there, and watch out for that green oozy substance. We recommend this only for archival storage.

ADDITIONAL FONTS

Ha! Fooled you! With the America Off-Line Word Processor, you just don't need additional fonts. It comes complete with unlimited fonts. Yes, not only does it have Times and Helvetica and Cairo, but it's got a whole lot more:

Hello!

Paramus, designed by 12-year-old Sally Schwabacher from New Jersey.

Hello!

St. Joseph's, designed by Dr. McKellan of Cincinnati, used primarily for prescription bottles.

GOODBYE!

Cabin, designed by Ted Kaczynski.

And that's just the start. There's also Flagstaff, Dead Sea, Pittsburgh, Erie and a whole lot more.

Spellcheck

America Off-Line members can purchase any one of several spellcheck systems, developed by such companies as Webster's, Funk & Wagnalls, Oxford and so on. These systems are far more comprehensive than most chintzy on-line spellcheckers, which is important, because many America Off-Line authors use slightly unorthodox spelling. Consider what happened when we ran some off-line text files through a Macintosh Spellcheck.

UPGRADING
THE PENCIL

Writers rejoice! The "pencil" isn't the only Word Processor out there on America Off-Line. Not by a long shot. Many members prefer something called the "pen." This fancy piece of hardware boasts more moving parts (to activate the printer, click the top button, much as you would a mouse), and a powerful editing function (White Out). And oh, the variety! You can buy anything from the Fountain Word Processor (a primitive version, sort of a TRS-80 of the group) to the Ballpoint Word Processor (the fastest of the line, equivalent to 25 megahertz). Be careful, though: "pens" can freeze up, just like your computer screen. So try to keep them out of the cold.

Even more complex than the "pen" is the "typewriter." This looks remarkably like your laptop, except it has "paper" instead of a screen. Listen for the satisfying "Bing"—much less irritating than the "Wild eep" you're used to.

And what if you can't afford any of these models? America Off-Line has even cheaper Word Processors for you. You can choose from the Stick-in-the-Dirt 3.0 (especially good for football diagrams), the Finger-with-Blood 486 (for death threats) and the Full-Bladder-On-Snowy-Day 8080 (for boys writing their names).

Call me Fishmeal.

—Herman Melville,
in *Moby Dick* (or Mob Dick)

Wham, that April with his shoppers sooty
The draught of March hat perked to the rotor.

—Geoffrey Chaucer (or Chancre),
The Canterbury Tales

Twas bridling and the shifty doves did gyro and
gumbo in the whale.

—Lewis Carroll (Chariot), *Jabberwocky*

See? It's just not the same.

The Trash

The Trash icon

This is very similar to the on-line Trash receptacle. But off-line, it's even more important to empty the "trash" regularly, especially if you use it for files such as Half-Eaten Sloppy Joe or Three-Day-Old Moo Goo Gai Pan. Also, try not to drag things to the off-line "trash," or you'll leave a liquid trail of refuse and your spouse will yell at you.

THE PEOPLE CONNECTION

Despite America Off-Line's sophisticated technology (pencils, staplers, etc.), our service is, above all, about people. We like to think of ourselves as one big community—the perfect place to meet folks who share your interests, hobbies and hygiene habits. At any time of day or night, literally millions of folks are hooked off, ready for you to join. So what are you waiting for? Let's learn how to interface!

Chat Rooms

Perhaps the most exciting and popular way to interact on America Off-Line is through our chat rooms, known in Reality as "parties." This is where several members get together in a "room" and exchange ideas, opinions, jokes or whatever. How do you access chat rooms? Just as you would in cyberspace, you first enter the America Off-Line Lobby area. After that, simply point and click the Elevator button, which takes you to the "party" itself.

Once inside the room, you are ready to begin interacting. Remember, leave a comfortable space

between you and your chat partner—about the distance you normally put between you and your monitor. And then start sending messages with your personal Soundcard, located in your throat. (Just as CAPITAL LETTERS are discouraged in cyberchats, you should try to modulate your off-line sound volume, unless you're in Texas.)

Sound like fun? You bet it is! But be careful. Although "parties" are basically similar to on-line chat rooms (i.e., friendly people, constant conversation), they also have their own peculiar set of rules, etiquette and protocols. Be sure to memorize the following:

RULE 1. Do *not* describe yourself. This may be difficult at first, but it's very important. Consider this transcript taken from a recent "party."

Member 1: "Hiya there. I'm a five-foot eleven vixen with a foxy body, silky thighs, and deep blue eyes."
Member 2: "No, you're a short, acne-faced guy."

You see, Member 1 (obviously an America Off-Line newbie), didn't realize that at a "party," the person with whom you're talking is actually IN FRONT OF YOU, looking right at you. This means a) you don't have to describe yourself, and b) if you do, you can't lie about what you look like.

RULE 2. Chat with a maximum of three members at a time. Part of the fun of being in an on-line chat room is typing in your message ("Vendela is so hooooooooottttttt!") and having all 23 participants read it simultaneously. At a "party," however, not everyone is interested in your thoughts on the Scandinavian supermodel. They're even less interested in your opinions about which *Deep Space Nine* cast members had extensive orthodontia.

RULE 3. Try to think of something *interesting* to say. This will also seem curious to newbies. After all, an above-average on-line conversation goes something like this:

Zapper404: "I eat soup."
PicardBoy: "Me too."

Strangely enough, this wouldn't cut the conversational mustard on America Off-Line. When speaking in Reality, it's recommended you have something on your mind *before* you open your mouth. Of course, many people break this rule—and for some reason, they always end up sitting one table over at Red Lobster (see "Fun & Games," page 48). Which brings us to our next important point.

RULE 4. Keep your secrets secret. "I can only become aroused when thinking of Jamie Farr in a vat of mango chutney." The Internet is filled with such confessions, happily announced under a pseudonym. At a party, however, there is no Anonymous function. Farr fetishism may get you tossed onto the street.

RULE 5. Focus, focus, focus. We all know that in an on-line chat room, a comment about Ugandan politics could be followed immediately by one on the importance of pimento loaves in the daily diet and no one would think it was strange. In fact, it's the norm. This is partly because there are so many people talking at once, and partly because users type in whatever crosses their minds. But on America Off-Line, conversations usually unfold "logically." In other words, try to respond directly to what your chat partner has just said. To help you, we present the WRONG way to conduct a party conversation:

Mike: "My name is Mike."
Susan: "Hi, Mike, how are you?"

Mike: "My voice coach is gay."

Susan: "I see." [*Awkward pause.*] "And what do you do for a living, Mike?"

Mike: "Women often feel better after a bubble bath."

Susan: "Um. That's probably true.... And how do you know our hostess Jennifer again?"

Mike: "I've only been to Green Bay twice. It sucked."

Susan: "You know, John, I'm kind of thirsty. I'm going to—"

Mike: "I'm a carpenter by trade. Cabinets mostly."

Susan: [*Relieved.*] "Oh. So that's what you do for a living. Do you like it?"

Mike: "MY VOICE COACH IS GAY!!!!!"

Susan: "Excuse me. I've really got to get some punch."

Now here's the RIGHT way to do it:

Mike: "My name is Mike."

Susan: "Hi, Mike, how are you?"

Mike: "Fine, and yourself?"

Susan: "Great. What do you do for a living?"

Mike: "Well, I'm a carpenter. I make a lot of cabinets."

Susan: "Really? That must be interesting."

Mike: "MY VOICE COACH IS GAY!"

Well, almost. But it's certainly an improvement! In a few weeks, Mike (known in cyberspace as doctor-whom) will be speaking just like an off-line pro.

RULE 6. No lurking. When we're on-line, we've all experienced the joy of hanging out invisibly in the background, listening to others yak it up. Well, unfortunately, on America Off-Line, "lurking" is much more difficult, and sometimes illegal. First of all, it's very hard to remain invisible. Camouflage doesn't work very well. Just try wearing an Army-green jumpsuit to your friend's baby shower. Or try donning a more sophisticated disguise—say, a pair of pants covered with pictures of Ritz crackers and pigs in a blanket. You still probably wouldn't blend into the background. Remember: You've got a three-dimensional body. So if you spend all night hovering near a conversation circle without ever talking, you'll hear such comments as: "Who's Jeffrey Dahmer over there?" Later, you may receive what's called a "restraining order" in the Mail (see "Using Mail," page 31).

Take two moments to absorb these rules. And when you're ready to move on, read these chat room FAQs.

Q: *I read in alt.urban.folklore that more than 23 people can fit in a single off-line chat room. Is this true?*
A: It depends on the size of the chat room. If you're going to a black-tie chat room at the convention center, you'll be in the same space as literally hundreds of other people! But try squeezing that number in a one-bedroom rent-controlled apartment, and you'd be at risk of a meltdown (aka "fire hazard"). To keep the number of people in check, most parties require you to have a password, or "invitation," from the off-line Host. (The Host is the one with the strained smile asking people to smoke outside.)

Q: *How do I leave a "party"?*
A: Another good question! As you know, leaving an on-line chat room is a snap. If you get bored or uncomfortable, you click the Exit button and you're gone. Maybe, if you're feeling charitable, you type "Bye." Off-line, however, things are a little more complicated. Before exiting a party, you must engage in the Off-Line Exit Procedure. The first thing you should know is that the truth is not always a good idea. It may be honest to tell the host "I'm leaving because your party sucks," but it's an easy way to get taken off future invitation lists. Instead, try one of these phrases:

Excuse: "I'm sorry I have to go, but the baby-sitter has to be back by eleven."
Translation: I'm bored.

Excuse: "Well, look at the time! I've got an early day tomorrow."
Translation: I'm really bored.

Excuse: "I have to go search for the lost continent of Lambdoon and retrieve its hidden treasures."
Translation: I'm unstable and should not be around other people.

When leaving an off-line chat room, you also probably want to make a comment about some aspect of the "party," whether it is the hostess's dress or the main course served at dinner. Your comment, of course, varies from situation to situation. Consider:

The situation: The rice pilaf was delicious.
The good-bye: "The rice pilaf was delicious!"

The situation: The rice pilaf was okay.
The good-bye: "The rice pilaf was delicious!"

The situation: The rice pilaf made you dry heave from across the room.
The good-bye: "The rice pilaf was delicious!"

Q: *What if I want to go to a Private Room?*
A: Off-line, going to a Private Room (known as "going back to my place") is a very big step. Unless the other person gives you very clear signs (rapidly batted eyelashes, a "gun" in the pocket), you should *not* ask to meet there. For more on Private Rooms, see "Sex & Romance," page 74.

Q: *How can I make someone stop talking to me?*
A: Use the Block function, called "walking away."

> ✔ **HOT TIP:** Want to try the latest, hippest trend? How about popping by a chat room featuring flashy, customized avatars? Off-line, these are called "costume parties." Usually they are held on the last day of October. Before entering these unique three-dimensional environments, you can choose one of thousands of avatars: Judge Ito, Marge Simpson, or noted colonial activist Cotton Mather, if you want to confuse people.

Forums

No doubt about it: America Off-Line is just brimming with people who share your interests—whether it be cooking risotto or fixing grandfather clocks. In fact, for every specialized forum in cyberspace, there is a place on America Off-Line you can go to find similar conversations. Here's just a sampling:

ON-LINE FORUM	OFF-LINE ANALOG
Sixty-Plus Center	Denny's in Miami (mid-afternoon)
Howard Stern Suite	Cheap seats at a Rangers game
Teen Talk	In line at a Pauly Shore movie
Parents R Us	Bleachers of a Little League game
German Nook	Hard Rock Café on 57th Street
Starfleet Academy	High school math club meeting

Mormon Talk	The seat next to you on a transatlantic flight
Kids' Corner	Neverland Ranch
Conspiracy Chat	Buchanan 2000 headquarters
Hollywood Tonite	Your cubicle area at work
Mercedes-Owners Madness	Local yacht and racquet club
Ayn Rand Connection	Freshman dorm room

Auditoriums

America Off-Line has so many notable and quotable members, we decided it would be fun to give regular folks like you a chance to interact with them. That's why we created the Auditorium feature.

Go to the Auditorium, and you'll get real-time images and audio bites from the day's featured speaker, whether it be a professor of botany or a disgraced politician.

There are, however, a couple of differences from on-line auditoriums. First of all, "chatting in rows" is strongly discouraged. And secondly, you'll rarely find Hollywood celebrities giving lectures in the Auditoriums. This isn't to say the stars don't enjoy Reality. It's no secret that dozens of Hollywood denizens from Tom Hanks to Dana Plato are members of America Off-Line. But celebs seem to prefer interacting with fans in more informal, spur-of-the-moment forums. Such as this one:

Fan: "Hey, look! It's Tom Cruise! Hey, Tom!"
Tom Cruise: [*Nods*]

Fan: "Hey, Tommy Boy! Over here, man!"
Tom Cruise's security man: "Please step away from the limousine."
Fan: "Nicole Kidman is hot!"
Security man: "Please move along, sir."
Fan: "Hey, Tom—I loved *Cocktail*! Can you really shake up a piña colada behind your back?"
Security man: "That's enough, buddy."
Fan: "Tommo, know what your best movie was? *Losin' It*. Just between you and me: Did you really do it with Shelley L—-ooooooooof!" [*Sound of body hitting the pavement.*]

See? It may not be quite as efficient as joining a conference, but it sure can be fun. At least for the security guard.

Speaking of celebrities, you're no doubt familiar with the Web's fan-created celebrity pages—the kind filled with, say, Alicia Silverstone images, Alicia Silverstone trivia, and rambling essays about the exact makeup of Alicia Silverstone's DNA. On America Off-Line, we have people who do similar things. They're called stalkers.

User Directories

Suppose you have made a "friend" at one of the chat rooms, and you want to locate her later. Fear not! America Off-Line provides literally dozens of user directories. In off-line lingo, these are called White Pages, and a copy of one can be found somewhere in your apartment, perhaps near the telephone, the thing that hooks up to your modem.

Some members are shy and leave themselves out of the Member Directories. If you must contact these people, ask for help from a customer relations specialist such as a private detective, a collection agency

or a hit man, depending on the situation (see "Help!" page 101).

Member Profiles

Curious to find out more about a particular member? Check out America Off-Line's member profiles, found in text files called High School Yearbooks. You'll learn all about their interests—whether they be debating or chess or football. The only problem with High School Yearbooks is that they aren't updated very regularly, if at all. You'll find profiles dating back to the Roaring Twenties, with interests such as "Doing the Charleston" or "Silent Cal impersonations."

Luckily, America Off-Line offers another type of member profile. These are called Biographies, and they can be accessed at the "library." Biographies are much more exhaustive than High School Yearbooks—some are literally hundreds of pages long, covering everything from the member's first breastfeeding session to her cousin Kathy's favorite Broadway musical. But these too have a downside. Not every member has a biography. Since it's very labor-intensive to put one of these together, they are generally reserved for members who have either created a great work of art or killed a lot of people in battle.

Beyond Smileys: Off-Line Emoticons

Suppose you're having a conversation, and someone says something amusing or flattering. We all know what to do on-line—you simply type in the smiley :). But in an off-line chat room, you just won't have access to a keyboard. How do you show you are happy? Don't panic. Expressing emotions off-line isn't as hard as you might think. For happiness, simply take the emoticon :), rotate it 90 degrees clockwise, and imitate the shape of the parenthesis with your mouth. This is a "smile" (not smiley, just smile). Herewith a guide to some other emotions:

SADNESS
What it is: Your hard drive just crashed, and you lost your canonical list of blond jokes.
Off-line equivalent: You just got a divorce.
Imitate : ((*Tip:* Don't forget to keep your head straight!)

ANGER
What it is: Someone sent you a flame reading "Bite me!"
Off-line equivalent: You just got fired from your job for no apparent reason.
Imitate >: (

JOY
What it is: You just traded e-mail with David Duchovny.
Off-line equivalent: You just watched the birth of your daughter.
Imitate :D

JEALOUSY

What it is: Your friend has Windows 95 and you don't.

Off-line equivalent: Your friend has a window office and you don't.

Imitate   /:(

SHOCK

What it is: Your laptop ran out of memory.

Off-line equivalent: You just found your husband in bed with another man.

Imitate   :-o

BOREDOM

What it is: You're waiting to download free art.

Off-line equivalent: You're listening to your aunt describe her bursitis.

Imitate |-O

INDIFFERENCE

What it is: You just read a newsgroup post about the wonders of the Great Lakes.

Off-line equivalent: You just read a magazine article about the wonders of the Internet.

Imitate   :/

LUST

What it is: You've just downloaded a hot-n-heavy Jennifer Aniston GIF.

Off-line equivalent: You just danced the last dance at your senior prom.

Imitate   :-P

LOVE

What it is: The feeling you have for the Ren and Stimpy Home Page.

Off-line equivalent: The feeling you have for your spouse.

Imitate   [[[[]]]] (This time, use your arms!)

Talking the Talk

When you wander into an America Off-Line chat room, you might be baffled. Our members can sound very strange. Often, they'll use long, complete sentences without a single acronym. Fear not. Here's a translation of what your off-line friends might have been saying to you.

Phrase:	In my humble opinion
Translation:	IMHO
Phrase:	Great minds think alike
Translation:	GMTA
Phrase:	Laughing out loud
Translation:	LOL
Phrase:	By the way
Translation:	BTW
Phrase:	Let's take a walk
Translation:	LTAW
Phrase:	No really, I'm talking to you.
Translation:	NRITTY
Phrase:	Hell-ooo? Can you get a life, please?
Translation:	HCYGALP?
Phrase:	I'm not kidding anymore. Turn off the freakin' computer right now or you're sleeping on the couch!
Translation:	INKATOTFCRNOYSOTC!

USING MAIL

Even as we speak, millions of people are trading messages through America Off-Line's popular and revolutionary method of communication: Mail. That's right, Mail. Without the "e." It's no typo! So named because our system isn't electronic, it is composed of a complex mixture of ink and gummy stuff and dangerously overworked human beings. (No type of mollusk is involved, despite a rumor propagated by alt.urban.folklore.)

What that means is this: When you sign onto America Off-Line, you'll get unlimited "mail" delivered every day (except Sundays) by a real person in a cute little uniform. Sound exciting? Read on.

The Components Of Mail

Although Mail is relatively user-friendly, you'll need to familiarize yourself with its several different features.

Message. Also called the "letter," the message is written on a piece of "paper" (see "The Desktop," page 10) and compressed for easy transmission (i.e., folded twice).

Envelope. This handy device holds the message. It looks remarkably like the envelope icon on your screen, but there's a big difference. With this envelope, you must lick the inside to seal it. Imagine the jolt you'd get if you stuck your tongue on your computer screen! Or maybe you already know—you dirty dog! (See "Sex & Romance," page 74.)

Address. Just as in cyberspace, every America Off-Line member gets his or her own unique Mail "address." Here's a breakdown of a typical one:

Jennifer Fensterblau
This is the member's User Name. (Remember: No @ sign!)

118 Meadow View Lane
This part (the "street address") is designed by an elite coterie of real estate agents and local government officials. They've made sure each part means something. For instance, "Meadow View" means that you have a glorious panorama of a Circle K parking lot. "Lane" means you'll be awakened every night at 3:00 a.m. by eighteen-wheelers that sound like they're driving through your bedroom closet. (To find out your "street address," simply walk outside your door and look at the number on your house.)

Buffalo, New York 14240
This is the home system, top-level domain, and a bunch of routing numbers.

Queue. Off-line, this is called a "mailbox," and it's located just outside your door, a few feet from your computer terminal. Be sure to delete or store your

Mail, or else your queue will get stuffed, and your neighbors will think you're dead.

Server. This is called the "Post Office." If you like dealing with volatile government employees, you can go to the server yourself and send off your Mail there. Otherwise drop it in one of the mini-servers located on street corners.

How Mail Works

Many America Off-Line members are mystified by the seemingly magical world of Mail. Well, it's not as complicated as you might think. Take a look:

1. When you place your envelope into the Mailbox, it drops at LIGHTNING SPEED to the top of the pile.

2. It sits there for about 17 hours.

3. The Mailman picks up your letter, puts it in his bag, and drives off toward the Post Office at LIGHTNING SPEED!

4. The Mailman stops for a prune Danish.

5. The Mailman arrives at the Post Office and immediately takes the rest of the day off to attend a Stress Management Seminar.

6-14. Lots of complicated stuff happens, including plenty more piles, two more prune Danishes, and a trip to South Dakota, where it is discovered the address is actually South CAROLINA.

15. Your letter appears in the addressee's personal queue, just 23 days after it was sent!

Advantages of Mail over E-Mail

Once you start using Mail, you won't believe you ever lived without it. Its benefits are legion. For instance, have you ever said, "The check's in the e-mail"? Hopefully not. But the relaxed pace of our system makes delaying payment a breeze. Another useful phrase is this one: "Oh, it must have been lost in the mail." Who could blame you? (By the way, some of our members jokingly refer to e-mail as "gale mail," a derogatory reference to the faster-than-the-wind speed at which it travels.)

Mail also enables you to send more than simple ASCII text. You can even send more than images! To make your message more special, how about enclosing a lock of hair, a dried flower, or a goat's heart with a dagger stuck through it? I can't count the number of times I've used that one!

The Message

Before writing the message section (the "letter"), you'll need to learn some protocols and etiquette of nonelectronic Mail. Let's take a look:

RULE 1. USE PUNCTUATION MARKS.
Experienced e-mail users may not be familiar with these handy little fellows, but in Mail, they're employed in almost every sentence. Let's see how these work:

Period: .
"I recently got a life."

Question mark: ?
"Can you believe I got a life?"

Comma: ,
"Believe it or not, I got a life."
By the way (BTW), you'll notice that Mail users also have the peculiar habit of using complete sentences—consisting of a subject, a verb, an object and all that jazz.

RULE 2. KEEP SIGS SHORT AND SWEET.

We all know the joys of ending e-mail letters with a trademark "sig"—a witty quotation or intriguing turn of phrase that goes right before your User Name. Well, America Off-Line members also have sigs, but they are quite a bit simpler.

On-line sig: "The Universe is laughing behind your back, Judy"
Off-line analog: "Sincerely, Judy"

On-line sig: "Sorry, that's not my emu, Judy"
Off-line analog: "Regards, Judy"

On-line sig: "I like whole wheat Twinkies in the morning! Judy"
Off-line analog: "Best wishes, Judy"

RULE 3. DON'T SEND A LETTER THAT READS "DOES THIS WORK?"

Just assume that it does. Otherwise, by the time you actually start exchanging content-filled letters, the polar ice caps will have melted, submerging the world in water.

Mail Addresses of the Rich and Famous

Not only regular people like you and me are using Mail. Many, many celebrities and industry titans are starting to use the system as well. So don't be afraid—fire off a letter to someone you admire. Here are some addresses:

The President
The White House
1600 Pennsylvania Avenue
Washington, D.C. 20500

Bill Gates
Microsoft
1 Microsoft Way
Redmond, Washington 98052-6399

Sandra Bullock
c/o Michaels & Wolfe
9350 Wilshire Blvd., Suite 328
Beverly Hills, California 90210

Patrick Stewart
c/o Star Trek-TNG Paramount
5555 Melrose Avenue
Hollywood, California 90038

And that's just a start!

Mail Security

Many of our members are concerned about the privacy of their Mail. It's a valid fear. Sometimes your letters *will* get read by others. This is especially true if the envelope is addressed to "The Evil Dictator Bill Clinton" or if the return address includes the words "Federal Penitentiary."

The good news is, America Off-Line offers a sophisticated encryption program, which, by applying complex mathematical transformations, makes data incomprehensible to the naked eye. If your letter is of a highly personal nature, we strongly recommend you run it through this program. To see how this works, look at this encrypted message from one of our members:

Dear Jenny,

Last night, Steve and I came close to having you-know-what! But he didn't have the whatchamacallit, so we didn't.

Love, Melissa

You're probably saying "Huh?" What the heck is User Name Melissa talkin' about? Well, with an America Off-Line de-encryption program, the meaning becomes clear as day:

Dear Jenny,

Last night, Steve and I almost played Jack-in-the-orchard. But he wasn't wearing a raincoat, so we didn't.

Love, Melissa

Or, to decode it even further:

Dear Jenny,

Last night, Steve and I almost made the chimney smoke, but he didn't have a balloon, so we didn't.

Love, Melissa

Got it yet?

Dear Jenny,

Last night, Steve and I almost did the horizontal polka, but he didn't have a shower cap, so we didn't.

Love, Melissa

All right. Moving on.

Payment Method

Instead of charging your credit card at the end of the month, America Off-Line Mail has a pay-per-letter method, the "stamp." This usually features the image of someone who has done something admirable for the country. Or Nixon.

Subject Lines

On e-mail, subject lines such as "Meeting Canceled" or "Eat Me" give a pretty clear indication of the contents of the message to follow. With the Mail system, things are a little more subtle. There is no subject line per se. But you can get the gist from a number of hints on the envelope.

Bad News. Your User Name is written "Anthony

James Brodsky Jr.," address window is transparent plastic, return address includes the words "billing" and/or "department," and the envelope features an "Urgent" stamp in red.

Good News. Your User Name is written "Cutie-Patootie Brodsky" in pink magic marker, and the return address includes the words "Your Personal Love Slave." The envelope smells like it's been soaked in Chanel No. 5 overnight.

Sending Copies

On America Off-Line, it's just as easy to send a dozen copies of a letter as it is to send one. Just ask your "secretary," available separately. (Note: Many of our members have opted for an upgrade on the "secretary" called the "assistant." The two are actually identical, except you don't need to buy your "assistant" flowers on Secretary's Day.)

Spamming

Just as in cyberspace, our Mail system is forever getting clogged with annoying info-junk. It's just one of those things. We even have our version of David Rhodes, of the notorious "MAKE MONEY FAST" chain letters. Ours is named Ed McMahon, and this guy promises unsuspecting Mail users that they may have already won a million dollars. Mr. McMahon could be the most despised member of America Off-Line, aside from Timothy McVeigh and David Copperfield.

Other insidious Mail users figure out your off-line profile and bombard you with offers. For instance, if you happen to subscribe to a vaguely liberal maga-

THE
TELEPHONE

If you get tired of sending Mail messages, America Off-Line offers another method of communication: the Telephone. This intriguing piece of hardware is very similar to your modem: it's hooked up to the same line and costs the same to use. Still, the Telephone is not a modem. Let's take a closer look at how it works:

Dialing out is easy. Simply extend your index finger and use the good old point-and-click method. Wait for the pickup. When that happens, you won't hear the high-pitched screeching sound you're accustomed to, unless you happen to be calling Fran Drescher. Instead, you'll hear a human voice saying "Hello."

Your response should be "Hello" as well. This is the equivalent of hardware handshaking.

At this point, you may encounter a filter called a "secretary" or "assistant" (see "Sending Copies," page 39). If this is the case, you'll have to give your User Name and password to gain access. However, you should know that the passwords are slightly different than those on-line. For instance, here are some passwords that will never work:

"I'm with the Amway Corporation."
"Tell her Cousin Ralphie's in town for the Pest Control Convention and he's ready to par-TEE!"
"We're calling about some unpaid parking tickets from 1982."

And here are some that just might work:

"Tell her I have some photographs of him in Palm Springs she'd be interested in."
"Yes, the Warren Buffett."
"We just got back the results of her chlamydia test."

A few on-line members are already familiar with the telephone. They've used the so-called Internet Phone to get low-cost long distance service. Well, America Off-Line also offers cheap service. Just go to Raoul around the corner and use his cell phone.

zine, you'll soon receive desperate letters from the Democratic Party, the ACLU, the Coalition for Bilingual Yield Signs, etc. It's almost as bad as cyberspace!

But perhaps the most unpleasant form of Spamming is called the Mail Bomb. One of America Off-Line's most vehement members, Ted Kaczynski, was well known for allegedly sending these. (He was so entranced by America Off-Line, he apparently neglected to ever set up a Web site.) In any case, those who have received Mail Bombs say opening them is even more annoying than getting ASCII art of the Olsen twins! If you suspect a package may be a mail bomb, do NOT open it. Immediately ask your assistant to open it.

Mail to the Outernet

Yes, America Off-Line provides Mail service to the Outernet. However, it costs a little more, and the chances of the message getting garbled (i.e., "lost") hover in the ballpark of, more or less, 100 percent.

Instant Messages

Just as with many on-line services, we have a system for sending immediate messages. Well, almost instant. Ours takes about a day, and is called FedEx.

REFERENCE TOOLS

If you're looking for information on almost any subject, you've come to the right service. We're pretty sure America Off-Line has the most powerful reference section around. Let's suppose for a minute that you loooove rigatoni. You can't stop thinking about it. You want to know everything there is to know about this delicious tubular little pasta. Well, you'll find America Off-Line has a treasure trove of rigatoni info—from its history to its ingredients to a list of notable rigatoni lovers.

But what if you couldn't care less about rigatoni? What if your passion is instead *vermicelli*? Fear not—we've got plenty of files on that too. But, you say, what about farfalle? Yes, farfalle as well! Penne? Yup. How about ziti? Um, nothing on ziti. Just kidding! Yes, there is LOTS of info on ziti too! So, in sum, we have lots of data on almost any subject under the sun. Including macaroni.

Databases

How can I access all this enlightening stuff? On America Off-Line, our text files ("books") are stored in massive databases ("libraries"). And we do mean massive! The largest, the Library of Congress, stores 700 million text files. Now, that's a big number—almost twice the amount Marc Andreesson earns on a good day!

The "libraries" are open to all America Off-Line members, and you don't need to use FTP to download files. Just bring proof that you live in the area, and you'll get immediate access. The data is kind of like shareware, except you have to return it when you're done, or else we'll revoke your borrowing rights. Then you'll have to download the files right there in the "library," next to the guy with a foot-long string of drool hanging from his lip ranting at you that Yasmine Bleeth is head of the Trilateral Commission.

With so much data, you may be nervous about finding the text file that's right for you. Well, fortunately, we provide a powerful search system, much like Lycos or Alta Vista. It's called the Card Catalog. So c'mon! Let's do a search!

1. Choose your topic. For the sake of this example, let's pretend you want to do research on gnocchi.

2. Go to the Card Catalog and discover that, yes, there are 435 text files on gnocchi, all located in section 378.2E.

3. Circle the library for about two hours looking for your section. Begin muttering.

4. Try to access Customer Support (known as the "librarian"). Notice the line is three hours long. Mutter loudly and clench fists.

5. Settle for an attractively bound book on aardvark life cycles.

See? Easy!

And now, for some Frequently Asked Questions (FAQs).

Q: *I've been downloading lots of America Off-Line text files, and I've noticed something very strange. Namely, where are all the smileys?*

A: Yes, it's true. America Off-Line authors rarely—if ever—use emoticons. So, you ask, "How should I know if the writer is happy or sad, joking or serious?" Well, believe it or not, you're supposed to infer his or her meaning from such intimidating-sounding concepts as context, tone, and style. Let's see how this works, using a text file from one of America Off-Line's finest authors, Charles Dickens.

> **It was the best of times.**
> **It was the worst of times.**

Could you figure out Dickens's intent? That's right.

> **It was the best of times :)**
> **It was the worst of times : (**

Not so hard, eh? To get you started, here are some other examples of writing with the emoticons left in. Compare these versions with the ones found in your Library.

> **And yes I said yes I will Yes :)**
> —James Joyce, *Ulysses*

> **Jesus wept : (**
> —The Bible

> **Elementary, my dear Watson ;)**
> —Arthur Conan Doyle,
> *The Memoirs of Sherlock Holmes*

All hope abandon, ye who enter here >:(
> —Dante Alighieri, *The Divine Comedy*

Note: When America Off-Line authors use exclamation points, it's usually only one at a time!!!!!!!! Ooops. I mean one at a time!

Q: *Are some text files harder to download than others?*
A: Indeed they are. Just like on your computer, some "books" are highly compressed, others not compressed at all. A highly compressed "book" would include anything assigned in the college course Tropes of Dual Modality: Aural Semiotics in Fin de Siècle Whales. Fortunately, America Off-Line offers a handy unstuffing program known as Cliffs Notes. And just as happily, there are plenty of off-line text files that don't need any unstuffing whatsoever. You can find these sold at the airport. In fact, most Jackie Collins files could be downloaded by an airplane pilot in mid-flight without endangering the passengers.

Q: *Which are the good text files? And which are a complete waste of time?*
A: That's a tricky one. No doubt you've heard the adage "You can't judge a CD-ROM by its packaging." Well, the same applies to "books." Often, you'll have to download the entire "book" before figuring out that it just plain sucks. Still, as with any adage, there are exceptions. The ground rules are these: Avoid anything with pictures of orchids on the cover; anything that quotes a review from the Oakley, Arkansas, *Ledger-Dispatch* instead of *The New York Times*, and, most importantly, anything by Robert James Waller.

Q: *Are there different types of databases?*
A: The short answer is "Yes." The longer answer is "Yes, there are." The really long answer is that the sheer variety of "libraries" is astounding. You can

OFF-LINE
FICTION

Talk about novel! At the library, you'll find a unique and exciting form of fiction. It's called non-hypertext fiction, and it flows linearly from one page to another instead of jumping around all over creation. Here's a hot list of some "novels" we recommend.

PORTNOY'S COMPLAINT. A look at cybersex in the precomputer age. (Then called simply "masturbation.")

THE GRAPES OF WRATH. A tale of the struggling business community in California before Silicon Valley came to the rescue.

THE SCARLET LETTER. A woman gets a big red "A" printed on her chest. (Times Roman, 48 point.)

MOBY DICK. Similar to a posting on alt.support.obsessive-compulsive.

BEOWULF. Kind of like Dungeons and Dragons and other fun role-playing games, except the outcome is always the same.

ON THE ROAD. Tales from the Noninfo Highway.

METAMORPHOSIS. As the name suggests, a precursor to "morphing." The main character turns into a noncomputer bug.

THE ILIAD. The tale of the original Trojan Horse—the kind that infects cities instead of hard drives.

INVISIBLE MAN. A Sandra Bullock–free version of *The Net*. The hero (like Sandra) discovers he has no social identity.

FAUST. A man gets some intriguing new data, but it sure wasn't shareware! The price was US$<his soul>.

choose from libraries specializing in science or medicine or law or business or what have you. You can even start your own personal "library," tailor-made to your interests, which you store conveniently on your "bookshelf" and never, ever disturb.

> **HOT TIP:** Newbies might want to check out *Walden*, the ultimate off-line text file. It's about a man who lives by a pond for a couple years with no computer, no modem, not even a beeper—and he survives! He's so unplugged, he doesn't order clothes from http://www.llbean.com—he actually sews his own shirts! He gets no deliveries from http://www.cheeseofthemonthclub.com—he grows his own turnips! You get the idea. It goes on like this for 246 adrenaline-pumping pages.

The Encyclopedia

Most libraries have another important reference tool: the "encyclopedia." Perhaps the best part about the encyclopedia, aside from its imitation leather cover, is that it is multimedia—just like a Compton's CD-ROM. Let's see how this works. Suppose you're interested in, say, tortellini. Well, go to the T section of your encyclopedia and look it up, where you'll get to read intriguing text about its long Italian history. But wait! You want to SEE what the tortellini looks like. Simply click your eyes to the right of the text, and there may well be a photo for you to enjoy. But wait again! Now you actually want to TASTE the tortellini. That's available too. Simply tuck the encyclopedia under your arm, sneak out to an Italian restaurant, and order up a bowl. Delicious!

FUN & GAMES

The *f* in America Off-Line stands for "fun!" (The other *f* also stands for fun, making it twice as much fun.) In plain English, that means that Reality won't just fulfill your data and communications needs but will also keep you amused and entertained for hours at a time. Take a look at what we've got.

Games

Believe it or not, some games require no monitors, no modems, not even a joystick. These intriguing off-line games come in several varieties:

Multi-User Dungeons

Perhaps the most popular MUD on America Off-Line is called Bingo. In this game, as many as 200 people can play at the same time, depending on the size of the Dungeon (aka "church basement"). Unlike most MUDs in cyberspace, however, Bingo has no goblins or trolls. Although the people playing can be pretty ugly.

Other Role-Playing Games

Another fun role-playing game is called charades.

Again, players rarely pretend to be a medieval wizard, but instead pretend to be "somebody with their arms flailing around" or "a guy having a seizure" or "what the hell what are you trying to do?"

And kids, they love their role-playing games too! They enjoy such classics as Cowboys and Indians, Cops and Robbers, and House. But parents should be careful of a certain role-playing game called Doctor, which would probably be banned by the Communications Decency Act. (For more games for children, see "Kids' Stuff," page 61.)

Strategic Fantasy Games

America Off-Line has plenty of games that require just as much forethought as Sim City. In one called Monopoly, apparently modeled on Bill Gates, you try to buy up all the real estate in Atlantic City without getting investigated by the Justice Department. This game needs to be updated frequently, as the equipment always seems to be disappearing into the couch, or your child's lower intestine.

Splatter Games

Some of our members go into the woods with paint guns and play a three-dimensional version of Virtua Fighter. Other members (e.g., the Marines) prefer to play their splatter games with even more realistic firearms and bigger playing fields, such as the Middle East.

Images

Just as the Internet stores thousands of JPEGs and GIFs, America Off-Line offers a smorgasbord of eye-pleasing images. Ours can be found in a massive databank called the Museum, and they can be visually downloaded in no time at all. Here's a look at some of the main formats:

IMPRESSIONIST
These are extremely low-resolution images. Do not complain to the museum staff. There's nothing they can do.

RENAISSANCE
These are nude binaries. Surprisingly, not a single one is of Teri Hatcher!

DADAISM
These are similar to images of flying toasters and the like.

PRIMITIVISM
Originally uploaded onto cave walls, these images look a lot like ASCII art.

OP ART
These are three-dimensional virtual images, and you don't need a helmet to view them!

> **CAUTION:** The binaries in the "museum" are NOT shareware. Do not try to download them off the wall and walk outside. If you must have copies for your desktop, you can buy them at the Gift Shop site. They're called Greeting Cards, and a batch of 12 will cost you about US$350.

Noninteractive Movies

America Off-Line has dozens of movies, displayed on screens roughly 8,000 times the size of your monitor. The most important thing to remember about off-line movies is this: They are NOT interactive. Unlike CD-ROM movies, the movies in Reality require nothing more of the audience than that they sit in their seats, chew popcorn, and sip Diet Coke. A disturbing number of our members find this confusing, and feel the need to shout suggestions to the characters. This is a waste of energy. Just consider the movie *Casablanca*.

Audience input: "Get on the plane!"
Outcome: Ilsa gets on the plane.

Audience input: "Don't get on the plane!"
Outcome: Ilsa gets on the plane.

Audience input: Complete silence.
Outcome: Ilsa gets on the plane.

Yes, Ilsa will always get on the plane. And Atlanta will always burn. And Mistress Natasha will always make her pleasure slave lick her thigh-boots. Oops. Please disregard that last one.

Slightly More Interactive Movies

If you just can't stand sitting back, if you feel you really do NEED to interact, why not try something called a Television? The Television will feel familiar to cyberveterans: You'll be looking at a screen the size of your monitor, and just as with the Web, you can waste hour after hour surfing the system without noticing the passage of time. You'll find the Television has dozens of addresses (aka "channels"), each of which has a series of "programs," most of which are produced by Aaron Spelling.

But the Television is not the Web. First of all, Television's superior technology provides continuous full-motion video with little image interruption (except for commercials). And with Television, you rarely have to download video of some guy eating Frito-Lays in his dorm room, unless you're watching public access.

Admittedly, the computer world still has some advantages. Television can't compete with the CD-ROM's level of interactivity. While watching *Beverly Hills 90210*, for instance, you can't decapitate Ian Ziering with a machete. But you can at least shut him up, by pressing the Mute button.

For true interactivity, you'll have to try a system called the VCR. This magneto-optical drive for video storage allows you to manipulate characters to your heart's content. If you want to hear Meryl Streep repeat the word "dingo" 18 times, just click on Rewind. If you want to turn *NYPD Blue*'s Detective Sipowicz into a Keystone cop, click on Search Forward. It's a great system, but as millions of blinking clocks indicate, it's as hard to figure out as DOS.

Wine and Dine Off-Line

No doubt it's fun to search on-line databases and discover the hottest new mouthwatering restaurants in town. But America Off-Line takes this concept even further. On our service you can actually *go to* the restaurants themselves!

When you enter a restaurant and get seated, your first task is to try to connect with your "server." This might be a challenge. Just like servers in the computer world, these are often busy or unavailable. But when you finally do connect, you'll get a pleasant surprise: restaurants are menu-driven systems. No doubt, the menus are a little strange, a little on the wordy side. For instance, your Macintosh menu probably wouldn't describe "Save" as "a delightful mélange of documents served with a side dish of hard drives and sun-dried file formats." Still, restaurant menus work almost like those on your screen. Simply point-and-grunt at your desired option. Within the next few hours you should be served your food.

And what kind of food are we talking about? Generally, the food at restaurants is different from the stuff you munch while surfing the Net. You'll find nary a Peanut Butter Crunch, Ramen Noodle with Thousand Island, or Cheddar Goldfish dipped in Nutella. Nope. You'll find a wide range of professionally prepared dishes with exotic names like "Filet of Sole" and "Baked Alaska." Many of these delicacies have NOT been microwaved!

Sports

Everyone knows the pleasures of clicking onto one of cyberspace's Sports Forums and yammering away. Here you can voice your opinion on anything in the wide world of athletics, whether it be that the Mets suck this year, that the Mets really suck this year, or that the Mets couldn't suck more if they gave $5 million contracts to a bunch of Hoover vacuum cleaners and sent them out onto the field with long extension cords. Okay. Moving on.

Well, America Off-Line offers the same service! Just go to any of the following sites: bar, men's bathroom, fraternity house, gym, elevator, carpool, locker room.

But once again, America Off-Line goes that one step further. On our service, you can do more than just talk about sports. Yes sir. You can actually WATCH them! Simply go to the Stadium site and you'll get to see the baseball players throwing, catching, hitting and making cell phone calls to their lawyers. And as a special interactive feature, you can voice your opinion to the players themselves, such as "Hey, Cubs, you suck," or "Hey, Cubs, you REALLY suck," etc. Baseball's not your passion? Why not go and tell football players, tennis, cricket or curling players they suck? The choice is yours!

There's another aspect to sports on America Off-Line. It's called "participating." But we don't have to get into that advanced stuff here.

THE NEWS

Here's a newsflash! America Off-Line offers access to literally thousands of newspapers and magazines. Yes, we've got every publication you can think of—and some you couldn't! Let's break that down. Here are some publications you *could* think of: *Time, Newsweek, The New York Times* and so on. But what about *Bicycling* magazine? Could you think of that? Maybe. It's a popular sport. Well, how about *Spud*, the magazine for potato farmers? No way could you think of that! Or *Concertina and Squeezebox*, the comprehensive newsletter covering trends in accordions? I believe I've proved my point.

In any case, you can find a whole bunch of magazines and newspapers on America Off-Line to keep you well informed. Here's a rule of thumb: If it's available in cyberspace, there's probably an off-line version too!

Exciting Features

Though each off-line publication is different, almost all offer these, well, exciting features:

FREQUENT UPDATES

America Off-Line's newspapers are updated *every single day*—just like those in cyberspace—except for the occasional system failure (known as "paperboy oversleeping"). The magazines are generally updated weekly or monthly.

INTUITIVE SETUP

To navigate a magazine or newspaper, simply turn to the user-friendly Home Page, which is called the Table of Contents. Take a look, see what section interests you, and then jump to the appropriate page using the Lick the Finger and Flip function.

To make things even easier, many newspapers are split up into sections, much like those you'd find on-line. This way, you can customize your daily information retrieval. If you're only interested in sports, read the Sports Section and toss aside all others. Is the temperature your main passion? Simply extract the Weather Page.

HOT TIP: America Off-Line also offers instant weather updates 24 hours a day. These can be accessed by opening the window in your bedroom and sticking your hand outside. If it's warm, the weather is warm; cold, the weather's cold. Easy!

ARCHIVES

America Off-Line stores back issues of many magazines and newspapers. Just look on your bathroom floor, or maybe in your mother's basement, or even the "library," if you have nothing else to do.

SEARCHING CAPABILITIES

If you are trying to find news about a particular topic, you'll be delighted by America Off-Line's powerful search engine. It's called an "intern." To initiate a search, simply tell the "intern" the parameters. "Hey, would you find me that article that came out, like, three years ago on wild dogs in Aruba? I can't remember if it was in the *Wall Street Journal* or *People*. Or maybe I just heard about it at a cocktail party. And now that I think about it, was it dogs or opossums? Hmm. Anyway, something like that. Some sort of animal in some country. Would you find it?" The "intern" will spend the rest of the day looking, because he or she really, really wants a job.

PORTABILITY

Our publications are so light, they can be carried almost anywhere. (Most weigh less than 3.5 pounds—some Sunday newspapers excepted). You can read *Forbes* on your yacht. Or flip through *Cosmo* at the hairdresser's. Or read *Newsweek* at wherever it is that *Newsweek* readers might go. Or enjoy *Swank* in the bathroom with the door locked. Nuff said.

COLORFUL IMAGES

With America Off-Line publications, you can access sharp images with no more hardware than a decent set of eyeballs. And talk about fast downloading! There's practically no delay. This is especially helpful with the aforementioned *Swank* in the bathroom. And speaking of *Swank*, some magazines do occasionally compress images. These are called "centerfolds" and pull out to reveal a larger-than-your laptop graphic. You supply the adhesive for your locker.

AN INTERACTIVE SECTION

On America Off-Line, you the reader can express your opinions directly to the folks at the magazine itself. This is called the Letters to the Editor section! When you write a letter, it may even appear in the following edition. Of course, there's not room to print *all* the Letters to the Editor, so magazine editors must choose a small sample. How do you make the cut? There's no guarantee, but here's an example of a letter that might make it in:

Dear Editor:

Great job on your magazine! I especially liked the witty cover photo of Marcel the Monkey as our nation's first president! That wig gimmick will never outstay its welcome.

Cynthia

And here's one that probably wouldn't:

Dear Editor:

You succccccccckkkkkkkkk!!!!!

Assweed

Again, this one might work:

Dear Editor:

Kudos to your publication! I'm delighted to learn that Andie MacDowell isn't just a talented actress, but that she has very strong views on the capital gains tax! I never knew!

Marion

And this one wouldn't:

Dear Editor:

You guys succccccccckkkkk hard!!!!!!!

Flamethrower

You get the idea.

DISCUSSION GROUPS

Suppose you found that article on Princess Di's new colonic irrigation system particularly interesting. Simply turn to the woman next to you on the subway and say: "Can you believe this article on Princess Di's new colonic irrigation system? I find it particularly interesting.... Where are you going?"

MULTIMEDIA ADVERTISEMENTS

Many magazines such as *Vogue* and *Mirabella* offer cutting-edge perfume ads that include not only visuals and text, but exclusive off-line "odor bites." Of course, some members find these a bit distracting. To filter them out, use a piece of hardware called a clothespin.

How to Access News

A merica Off-Line offers three fun and easy methods.

SUBSCRIBING

This is very much like subscribing to an Internet mailing list, and gets your newspaper delivered right to your door. For those so inclined, America Off-Line provides an even more powerful downloader, which brings the paper right to your feet. Available at the ASPCA.

THE NEWSSTAND

This America Off-Line site offers a big old buffet of publications for you to browse free of charge before buying. But don't get carried away by this generous offer. Only browse a little. If you start filling out the *New York Times* crossword puzzle or clipping coupons from *USA Today*, for instance, you've browsed too much, and may get physically threatened by the owner.

THE GROCERY STORE

At this America Off-Line site, where you buy your Spam (see "Glossary," page 114), you can also download some news. Generally, the news is less about Bosnia and more about Spanish heartthrob Antonio Banderas's secret third nipple. This type of news is free, so long as you put it back before the cashier rings up your last can of Spam. Otherwise, you're stuck with it.

How to Delete News

Yes, we admit it. Disposing of off-line publications is a little tricky. The problem is that America Off-Line only has a limited amount of storage space, which forces us to do something called "recycling." What is recycling? Well, when they took the same old *Star Trek* concept and turned it into a supposedly new show (*The Next Generation*)—that was "recycling."

You can either let us recycle or do it yourself, by stuffing the *Los Angeles Times* into your catbox.

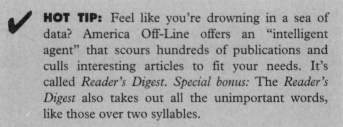

HOT TIP: Feel like you're drowning in a sea of data? America Off-Line offers an "intelligent agent" that scours hundreds of publications and culls interesting articles to fit your needs. It's called *Reader's Digest. Special bonus:* The *Reader's Digest* also takes out all the unimportant words, like those over two syllables.

KIDS' STUFF

Here at America Off-Line, we believe that children are the future. The future in my particular house had a bladder problem last night and put me in a very, very bad mood. But regardless, America Off-Line believes in children. And the exciting thing is, children seem to believe in America Off-Line, as well.

Right now, not only are kids enjoying our service in record numbers, but they are signing up at younger and younger ages! We have tykes who started using Reality just moments after emerging from the womb. And they take to it so well. It seems the prepubescent set isn't intimidated by Reality in the way many adults are, mostly because they haven't yet learned the concept of mortality. In any case, experts say that soon kids will be able to navigate America Off-Line better than their parents.

And it's no wonder they like it. Look at what's available:

Kids-Only Chat Rooms

Junior will love making "friends" with other young America Off-Line members in these exclusive chat rooms for kids, also called playdates (see "Popular Kids' Sites," page 65). Just listen to the fun these young members are having:

Child 1: "You're a sphincterhead!"
Child 2: "No, YOU'RE a sphincterhead!"

Um...wait a second. I'm sorry. That's actually an excerpt from the Rhode Island State Legislature, an adult chat room. But you get the idea.

Games

Junior can pick from dozens and dozens of nonvideo games on America Off-Line, accessible at the local Toys R Us site. There you'll find:

TETRIS
With this game (known off-line as Blocks), the challenge is for tykes to put geometric shapes together while resisting the urge to swallow them.

PHOTOSHOP
Kids love to fiddle and distort and rearrange faces with this program. It can be found under the name "Mr. Potatohead."

DOOM
With three-dimensional action figures (G.I. Joe, the Transformers, etc.), youngsters can create their own outer-space destruction scenarios!

AFTER DARK
Little Sally can enjoy a gorgeous, full-motion video pattern with the "kaleidoscope."

PAC MAN
The classic all-you-can-eat video game has had a rebirth off-line. It's called "Candyland."

MICROSOFT FLIGHT SIMULATOR
On America Off-Line, boys and girls love to run around the "backyard" with their arms outspread, shouting "vroom! vroom!"

POINTY STICK AND INSECT
This fun game has no direct analog online, but violent children will find it just as fulfilling as *Warcraft 2: Tides of Darkness*. It consists of jabbing at a bug with a twig, making it run for its life, letting it believe it has a chance, then squashing it to a fine paste.

Education

You want your kids to learn their ABCs? Memorize the multiplication tables? Well, we believe that America Off-Line offers the best educational forums in Reality. We call them Schools.

The School has exciting and challenging programs tailored for ages three on up. Way up. In fact, many adults on America Off-Line (called "graduate students") continue enjoying our educational forums well into their forties, prompting such questions as, "When are you going to get a job?" and "What's with that growth on your chin?"

But it's no wonder they like them. For America Off-Line educational forums are just about as interactive as CD-ROMS. Each "schoolroom" comes complete with an America Off-Line staff member, or "teacher," who asks the students thought-provoking questions in real time. Let's listen in on some samples:

SOCIAL STUDIES FORUM
Teacher: "Chloe, what is the capital of Peru?"
Chloe: "Uh....Can I go to the bathroom?"

HISTORY FORUM
Teacher: "Toby, when did the Civil War start?"
Toby: "Uh....Can I go to the bathroom?"

ENGLISH FORUM
Teacher: "Max, who wrote Huckleberry Finn?"
Max: "Oh, that's my beeper. Gotta go."

Note: America Off-Line offers two types of forums. You can choose between the free (aka "public") and pay-as-you-go (aka "private") educational forums. The main difference? The kids in pay-as-you-go forums generally pack handguns with a slightly lower caliber.

Parental Control Software

As you've seen from previous chapters, America Off-Line is mostly a friendly place. A community. But as with any community, there are elements that are not good. Or, to put it another way, bad.

Well, maybe not *bad*. That's a strong word, and we don't want to scare off any potential subscribers. Let's just say there are things on America Off-Line that you might not want your kid exposed to. After all, they're just kids! That's why America Off-Line is proud to offer the most extensive line of Parental Control software around. These programs filter out the off-line chaff, allowing your child to enjoy the noncyber wheat.

BEDTIME
Filters Out: Cheesy late-night movies on USA Network with babes in hot tubs.

HOUSE IN SUBURBS
Filters Out: Urban decay, poverty, car alarms.

HAND-HOLDING AND/OR LEASH
Filters Out: Speeding cars, old men offering "candy."

GROUNDING FOR A MONTH
Filters Out: Chat rooms with grain alcohol.

BLINDFOLD
Filters Out: Violence, pornography, light.

GUILT
Filters Out: Everything fun—and it can last a lifetime, too!

POPULAR
KIDS' SITES

Disneyland

Sandbox

McDonald's

Gymboree

Skating Rink

Summer Camp

The Foot of Their Parents' Bed at 6:00 a.m. with an
Interesting Clump of Dirt That Daddy Should Wake
Up and Look At

Enjoying America Off-Line With Your Kids

Just as some parents sit side by side with their kids at the keyboard, America Off-Line is full of features in which you can participate as a family. You can watch a noninteractive Disney movie, collaborate on a "letter" to Grandma, or even play an off-line game, Softball, which is loads of fun because children under ten aren't that hard to beat, especially if you wear cleats and slide into them really hard.

✔ **HOT TIP:** Are you tired of looking after your kids every second they're in Reality? Why not take a well-deserved break with the "organic" baby-sitter? This is an actual human being who, just like a Muppets CD-ROM, will keep your kids entertained all evening, at a cost of a mere US$5 an hour. The baby-sitter will read stories, play games and let the little tykes braid her hair. Unless, of course, she's too busy getting drunk on peach schnapps from your liquor cabinet.

LET'S GO SHOPPING

Suzie wanted to buy a dozen roses for her sweetie. Did she click onto the World Wide Web? Nope. She simply zoomed into one of the dozens of Flower Shop sites available on America Off-Line. Jerry needed a new striped tie for his business suit. Where'd he find it? At a Men's Clothing Store in St. Louis, far from the Information Highway. Lyle and Erik needed to find some sawed-off shotguns—and fast! Where'd they turn? That's right—Reality.

The truth is, America Off-Line is a shopper's paradise, bursting with literally thousands and thousands of outlets to choose from. The savvy consumer can meet almost all of his or her shopping needs without a single click of the mouse. (Of course, we don't recommend this, but it *is* possible.)

Accessing Off-Line Stores

America Off-Line comes complete with its own comprehensive Yahoo! directory of shops. It's called the Yellow Pages. Here you'll find that, just like businesses in cyberspace, each Reality store has its own address. For instance:

Bloomingdale
On-line address:
http://www.bloomingdales.com
Off-line address:
850 Lexington Avenue, New York, NY 10021

Neiman Marcus
On-line address:
http://www.neimanmarcus.com
Off-line address:
800 South Del Monte Drive, Dallas, TX 75217

Starbucks
On-line address:
http://www.starbucksusa.com
Off-line address:
Every mall, airport, and neighborhood in Reality. In fact, if you haven't checked your bedroom closet in the last few hours, you should look and make sure Starbucks hasn't opened an outlet there. Tomorrow, you'll probably be asking for "a decaf latte and my green blazer, please."

CAUTION! Most shops are not open twenty-four hours a day. Do not try to access them at 3:00 a.m. or you might end up in a Private Room at the state penitentiary (see "Danger! Danger!" page 84).

Special Off-Line Bonus Shops

Want more proof that Reality is becoming a force to be reckoned with? Here it is: Many businesses have decided to set up shop exclusively off-line, with absolutely no cyberspace presence whatsoever. For instance, Uncle Fudder's Bait and Tackle Shop off Route 19 in Birmingham cannot be found anywhere on the World Wide Web.

When we recently asked Uncle Fudder himself why Reality was the perfect site for his store, he explained he was a little too busy to answer questions right then. (Although he did find time to escort us from his shop using some down-home language and a baseball bat.) In any case, this seems clear: Uncle Fudder chose America Off-Line because it gives him excellent access to his clientele. Which, judging from our visit, consists of big-bellied guys who paint Confederate flags on their pickup trucks and have very powerful left jabs.

Customer Support

Another benefit of off-line shopping is the helpful customer support staff. Every store has at least one well-informed employee ready to answer your questions in *real time*. Just the other day, we accessed the Video Store, asked the staff member if he had a certain movie, and received instant feedback: "*The Maltese* WHAT? Never heard of it. How about *Meatballs 3*?" At our next stop—the bookstore—the help was just as immediate: "John Dos WHO? Maybe you mean John Grisham? We got lots of his stuff. *The Client, The Firm, The Rainmaker, The Paralegal, The Bailiff, The Alternate Juror....*"

Merchandise Descriptions

Just as with shops in cyberspace, our customer support staff provides handy descriptions of the available stock. Of course, America Off-Line's descriptions are usually more to the point. For instance:

On-line description: "Summer fun is only begin-
ning with these great shorts featuring Bugs Bunny
embroidery, a comfortable drawstring, and two pock-
ets. 100 percent cotton."

Off-line description: "You gonna buy that or
what?"

✔ **HOT TIP:** Newbies who haven't been outside in a
few years might want to shop for something called
"sun block." This is sort of like the protective
screen you put over your monitor, but this one
covers your entire body!

The Interactive Experience

Yes, we're proud of it. Shopping on America Off-
Line is pretty darn interactive. In fact, probably
more interactive than shopping in cyberspace. When
you're buying zucchinis, you don't merely look at a
binary image of them. You actually pick the vegeta-
bles up, squeeze them, and figure out if they're ripe.
When you're buying a tulip, you go ahead and take a
sniff! When you're buying a mattress, you lie down,
stretch out, take off your pants and then promise the
security guard not to come back.

Making the Transaction

Suppose you find something in the America Off-
Line shops that you actually want to buy. (And

FREE STUFF

As you know, cyberspace is packed with free software, free information, free images. Well, fear not. America Off-Line has plenty of free stuff as well. Here's just some:

Cheese cubes. At your off-line grocery store, get a toothpickful of sharp cheddar.

Shoes. The ones that don't fit your older sister.

Advice. "That jacket is a little too big in the shoulders." "You should part your hair on the other side." "Stop following me or I'll call the police." And other gems.

Harassment. If you are a woman, go to Ladies' Nite at the local bar.

Trips to the Caribbean. Simply get elected to Congress and you'll enjoy free "conferences" in Jamaica sponsored by the Association of Plastic Cutlery Manufacturers.

Newspapers. Download the "alternative weekly" for free from little metal boxes on the street corner. Sometimes there's even an article or two squeezed in between the ads for 976 numbers.

Bathrobes. They come free with a deluxe hotel suite.

Magazines. Sign up for a free six-week trial subscription. After that, if you want to discontinue, well, you can't.

Toasters. Just open an off-line bank account!

Fresh air. Go outside, look around at the trees, and take a deep breath. Your credit card will not be billed!

who wouldn't!) You can pay for your purchase with the traditional method well known to cyberspace veterans—the credit card. Or you can use something unique to Reality: cash.

The off-line substitute for your credit card number...cash

This piece of green "paper" usually has the picture of a former America Off-Line CEO on the front. (For those who don't follow these things, the CEO is the boss to Al Gore, whom you know as the guy touting the Information Highway.)

Let's see how cash works.

Salesperson: "That scarf will be $19.50."
You: "Okay." [*Reading from a $20 bill.*] "Card number B4325052E. Expiration date: 1789."

Whooops! That's not how cash works. With cash, the salesperson needs more than the bill's serial number. He or she needs the actual, physical bill, which then gets stored in the Cash Register.

(Unlike the American Express Gold Card, cash has a limit. Five dollars for a five-dollar bill, ten for ten, etc.)

This security file is used to store cash.

After the purchase, you're in for another surprise. You don't go home and wait four to six weeks for delivery. You don't even wait overnight. America Off-Line offers shoppers INSTANT gratification. You actually grasp the lamp or scarf in your hands and walk out with it that day!

IMPORTANT REMINDER: When making a purchase on America Off-Line, you are NOT alone at
your keyboard in the privacy of your room. Nope—
there are other shoppers in the same physical space.
That means:

1. You should NOT try on that cool-looking pair of
corduroy pants in the middle of the store. Those
other customers may not want to see the number of
holes in your BVDs. Instead, at most America Off-
Line clothing outlets, you can use Private Rooms
called "fitting rooms." These not only give you a
chance to test out the pants, but also to examine
every fat roll and skin blemish on your body under
the 14,000-watt fluorescent lights.

2. If you are buying something of a slightly personal
or embarrassing nature (i.e., a tube of hemorrhoid
ointment, jock itch spray, the *Friends* theme song
CD), you should be as discreet as possible or risk the
withering stares of customers. The most popular
method, dubbed the Woody Allen method, is a bit
expensive but often the best bet. "I'll have some
Crest, some baking soda, Arrid extra dry, a dozen
bottles of Pine-Sol cleaner. Oh, and maybe, while I'm
here, a couple of those things behind the counter that
look like they might be useful for plant holders....
Yes, the lubricated ones...the ones with studs."

✔ HOT TIP: Want more information about a certain
toothpaste, motorcycle or microwave oven? Many
products have something very similar to a URL
number. It's called an 800 number, and often it's
printed right there on the product itself. Dial it up
and ask away!

SEX & ROMANCE

Who would have thought? When we started America Off-Line, we knew it would be a great information resource and a revolutionary way to communicate. We never expected we'd be playing Cupid! But sure enough, more and more of our members (no pun intended) are meeting and having romantic relationships sans computer. And here's one Ripley himself might not believe: We know of several members who have even gotten married without exchanging a single e-mail!

Hot Spots

As romance has become more popular off-line, we've set up dozens of sites for people to meet potential mates—sort of the off-line equivalent of the Flirt's Nook. They're called Singles Bars.

But many members don't restrict their searches to the Bars. They get the sparks flying (to use a familiar electronic term) at a regular old chat room, while downloading files at the "library," or in their Senatorial campaign headquarters. Of course, you should also know there are some off-line sites where romantic overtures are generally a bad idea. These include the Family Reunion and the Lamaze Class.

Pitching Woo

What's the protocol for meeting an off-line mate? Simply follow these simple rules and you should be okay.

RULE 1. A little subtlety goes a long way. For those who don't know, "subtlety" means refraining from shouting "ANY HORNY FEMALES IN THE ROOM?" as you would on-line. Instead why not start off with a little "small talk," about the weather, the latest current event, etc.

RULE 2: Instead of complimenting your own looks, compliment the looks of...your potential partner!

This will seem strange to cyberveterans. But believe it or not, flattery of your off-line chat partner works wonders. Take a look at how this is done:

On-line: "**I** have a love tool the size of the Eiffel Tower!
Off-line: "**You** have pretty eyes."

On-line: "**I** have breasts that would take you three days to climb!"
Off-line: "**You** look good in plaid."

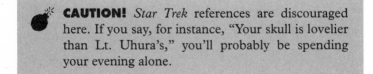

CAUTION! *Star Trek* references are discouraged here. If you say, for instance, "Your skull is lovelier than Lt. Uhura's," you'll probably be spending your evening alone.

Speaking of our members' appearances, we should tell you about one of the most exciting aspects of America Off-Line romance. Namely, the sheer variety of physical types on our service! As I'm sure you've noticed on-line, almost everybody looks pretty much the same. If they are female, they usually describe themselves as looking like Teri Hatcher. If they're male, they resemble Brad Pitt.

Not so off-line! Sure, you'll get the occasional doppelganger to Mr. Pitt, but just as often you'll encounter a guy who looks like Wallace Shawn with more back hair. And though some women do look like Teri, you get just as many who remind you of the "full-bodied" girl on *Facts of Life*, only with a deformed nose.

RULE 3: Do not ask someone's gender! In cyberspace, we're all familiar with that acronym MORF (Male or Female?). Well, on America Off-Line, this is not the best way to get the romance ball rolling. It's considered a big "turn-off," to use another electronic term. Instead, you should try to figure out your potential mate's gender without asking, using clues like body type, voice, and whether or not they regularly quote *The Three Stooges*.

Luckily, it's usually not a big problem. In fact, gender confusion is pretty darn rare in Reality. Why? Simply because it's much harder for men off-line to pretend they're women. Although possible, it takes considerably more time and effort. Consider:

Steps to becoming a transvestite on-line:

Step 1. Announce "I'm a girl!"

That's it! But now look at the steps to becoming a transvestite off-line.

Steps to becoming a transvestite off-line:

Step 1. Squeeze into an evening gown.
Step 2. Put on a big wig.
Step 3. Spackle on tons of makeup.
Step 4. Take a moment to call the president and warn you'll release the wiretaps of him having sex

with his mistress if he messes with your bureau (optional).
Step 5. Slip on high heels.
Step 6. Announce "I'm a girl!"

So you can see why Reality has many fewer transvestites. Still, there are times when you should be careful—for instance, if you're in Miami Beach, certain areas of New York's West Village, or a Benny Hill sketch.

Interfacing Without Clothes

Suppose your off-line woo-pitching is going along pretty well. You may soon be ready to take it a step further and engage in Computer-Free Cyber-sex—or, more simply, "sex." For this, America Off-Line provides thousands of Private Rooms. These are called bedrooms. (If you are between the ages of 17 and 21, other Private Rooms serve just as well. The Game Room, the Backseat of a Camaro, or a Dumpster Outside Stuckey's, for instance.)

When you get into your Private Room and onto the "bed," there are a few simple "sex" guidelines to remember. Let's examine these.

RULE 1. Use TWO hands. Yes, I know. That's one more than you're accustomed to. However, employing both your right AND left hands while having sex can double your pleasure. No doubt, you'll find it strange at first. Ease into it. For the first few times, pretend one hand is still on top of that old familiar keyboard. Try typing "Oh baby, oh baby" on your partner's shoulder blade.

RULE 2. There is no need to communicate everything that is going on as it is happening. Again, this will be peculiar to those accustomed to typing "I'm nibbling your ear" or "I'm massaging your thighs." But in "real sex," your partner will probably know without you saying anything! What's more, since real sex can get quite complicated, saying everything out loud might not sound so good and might even ruin the mood. Regard:

Him: "I'm massaging your silky thighs."
Her: "Mmmm."
Him: "Now I'm taking off your bra....I'm still taking off your bra....This seems to be a particularly tricky one. What is this, childproof?"
Her: "Would you just get it off already?"
Him: "Okay, the bra is off!...Hey, watch the lamp!"

You get the idea.

RULE 3. Sex in Reality often involves *different positions*. Again, this is quite different from cybersex. Cybersex has the position called "sitting in front of the computer." And that's about it. You can't exactly mount your Macintosh from behind or climb on top of your Toshiba—you wouldn't see the screen.

But on America Off-Line, there are dozens of positions for you to choose from. Dozens! Hard to imagine, isn't it? But some hardworking people have spent a long time trying. To see a more in-depth guide to this topic, access the "library" and download a text file called the Kama Sutra.

Real Sex Drawbacks

B efore diving into the exciting world of computer-free sex, please read about these potential dangers. (See also "Danger! Danger!" page 84.)

STDs. Just as too much cybersex can lead to carpal tunnel syndrome, too much noncybersex can cause these nasty fellows. To help prevent STDs, America Off-Line provides an important piece of software: the Condom. So just as you should always wear wrist guards when typing, you should always wear a Condom when having sex.

Children. These laptop-size creatures are miniature versions of you but a lot louder (see "Kids' Stuff," page 61). They take up a lot of time every day—more time than it takes to download, say, a dozen Dean Cain GIFs at 1200 baud. To prevent children, you can also wear the Condom.

Equipment failure. This happens every once in a while—especially to men, and especially as the equipment gets older, and especially if that bastard Kirchner got promoted to vice president last week even though he didn't deserve it one-tenth as much as you did.

The breakup. As opposed to computers, where you can simply stop responding to your partner's e-mails, things get a little dicier on America Off-Line. Get ready to learn about concepts such as "alimony," "Prozac" and "the Great CD Divide."

YOUR MONEY

If the *f* in America Off-Line stands for "fun" (see "Fun & Games," page 48), then the *m* stands for "money." Don't ask us what all the other letters stand for. The *f* and the *m* are the only ones that we needed. In any case, America Off-Line is the ideal place for managing your finances. Take a look!

Off-Line Banking

Believe it or not, you can do all your banking without ever clicking on your Quicken Deluxe. It's easy. Simply block out a little time—say a fortnight—and zip on down to the local branch of your bank. There, you'll see a screen (or Bullet-Proof Glass Shield), behind which are customer specialists who will tell you in real time that you've overdrawn a lot of money.

Don't have time for that? Neither do we. That's why America Off-Line offers an even more efficient and attractive banking program. It can be accessed by lifting up your mattress. Here you can make deposits, withdraw funds and check your balance, all in an instant! Plus, you'll sleep soundly, knowing your money is safe from hackers, as long as you don't get up to go to the bathroom.

Paying Bills

Paying bills is never fun. But neither is watching Andy Rooney jabber on for 12 minutes about wacky detergent names. Which isn't exactly relevant, but it certainly is true! In any case, paying bills is never fun, but you have to do it anyway. So why not try America Off-Line's time-tested bill-paying program?

The first thing you'll need is a check.

Checks are pieces of paper that often come adorned with colorful GIFs: a collection of birds, ships, or sunsets, for instance. (Sorry, Usenet users, no naked Denzel Washingtons.) Checks are extremely convenient. Generally, they are small enough to fit snugly onto your desktop, unless you just won a major tennis tournament, in which case your check won't even fit into the trunk of your limo.

Now take a Word Processor and input the name of the company you owe and the amount you owe, followed by your "sig" at the bottom. No need to add a funny ASCII drawing to your sig. It's enough to just scrawl your name illegibly. Zip it off in the Mail (see "Using Mail," page 31), and pray it arrives after your paycheck clears!

Stocks

Whether you want to dabble in the market with some leftover birthday money or engineer a hostile takeover and put thousands of people out of work, America Off-Line is the place for you. Among the stock services we offer:

Quotes. Get immediate access to the NYSE, NAS-DAQ, the Nikkei index and many, many others. Just look in your daily newspaper!

Transactions. Buy and sell shares without a single click of your mouse. Simply call an America Off-Line Stockbroker, who will register your order, then tell you a joke about the latest national tragedy.

Information. America Off-Line is filled with experts on the stock market. For instance, the guy who cuts my hair informed me for half an hour that biotech stocks are the next big thing, even though I thought I made it very clear I was engrossed by a *Field and Stream* article on trends in mud boots. If your barber isn't available, try another reliable program. It's called the Dartboard, and can be accessed in your basement Velcroed onto fake wood paneling.

America Off-Line Pricing

While we're on the subject of money, we thought we'd address America Off-Line's pricing structure. After all, we get a lot of questions about it, along with some complaints and not a few bomb threats. Here's the situation: We try to make Reality as reasonable as possible. As you noticed on the cover of this "book," your Starter Kit comes with 10 FREE hours of Reality. Not a bad deal. Use that time to explore the "library" or a chat room. (Remember to show people this book so they'll know you don't have to pay.)

But hold on. What we couldn't fit into that little balloon on the cover of this book is an even better deal. If you join America Off-Line early on in your life—say, at birth—you don't just get 10 free hours of Reality. You get 18 free YEARS of Reality. That's right: not a single bill to worry about. It's all paid for—just as long as you don't screw up and get kicked out of school for smoking some evil mary jane cigarettes under the stadium bleachers, in which case you'll have to support yourself, you bastard.

Once you've used up your free time, you will automatically be enrolled in our annual payment plan, called Taxes. Now it's true: We charge a tad bit more than your average on-line service. But we think we're worth it. If you disagree, you can tell a "federal judge," who is generally pretty understanding.

After taxes, you will be charged according to the number of premium services you enjoy. For instance, America Off-Line member Charlie Sheen recently enjoyed $50,000 worth of premium services at a site run by Heidi Fleiss. Go Charlie!

DANGER!
DANGER!

Just as even the best computer code always has a couple of annoying bugs, so too does America Off-Line have one or two unpleasant aspects. (Or, as you'll see in this chapter, four of them.) But this doesn't mean you should avoid Reality altogether! Just be prepared.

Viruses

These little suckers can get in your system and really do some damage. The most common off-line virus has the silly-sounding name of Influenza. But you won't be laughing if you catch it! Think about what Galileo did to some hard drives, but with a lot more mucus. Other viruses include Colorado Tick Fever, Rubella and Chicken Pox, which targets younger users. Fortunately, America Off-Line offers a wide range of "virus" protection software, all of which can be used separately or together. (See next page.)

Viruses and the Outernet

The Outernet can harbor some particularly nasty viruses, including one called Montezuma's Revenge. When on the Outernet, use common sense:

don't download any files such as Local Water or Clams on the Half Shell.

Flames

Most America Off-Line members are extremely civil, friendly and mature. Still, there will always

ANTI-VIRUS
PROGRAMS

Please install at least one of these before disconnecting from your modem and wandering outside on a cold day:

1. EARMUFFS
2. GLOVES
3. LONG JOHNS
4. SCARF
5. CHICKEN SOUP
6. VITAMIN C
7. FACE MASK
8. HERMETICALLY SEALED SPACE SUIT

But before you get too cocky, you should know that sometimes those tricky viruses can elude even the best protection programs. If this happens, we'll have to rebuild your system. In previous years, we sent an off-line customer support specialist (or "doctor") to your home, but now our service has grown too big, and besides, you might be a psycho. We now ask you to bring yourself in. Be warned: You might experience some delays. We apologize. A lot of people are looking for similar help. And we must be honest—things aren't going to be better in the near future. We're switching to a new system called "HMOs," which means the delays will be about as long as those on CompuServe's 800 number.

TERMS OF SERVICE

Here at America Off-Line, we don't joke around about our rules. For instance, we'd never say, "A rabbi, a priest and a Frenchman walked into a bar and ordered a list of America Off-Line rules." No, we're quite serious. To see a full list of rules, search in the library under file name Penal Code. You'll find we discourage lots of things: flames involving bloodshed; an activity called "shoplifting," which is akin to illegally pirating software; playing a hoax on investors (aka "fraud") and much, much more.

If you break our rules, be sure that we will take action in one of three ways:

•**Increase your user fees.** A member of the America Off-Line security team will give you a "speeding ticket" or a "fine."

•**Suspend you.** You'll be put in a Private Room and have to chat with another bad America Off-Line member for a few years. After a while, the conversations will get even less interesting than alt.fan.tolkien.

•**Terminate your service.** This is only for very serious cases, and imposition varies from state to state. In recent years, there have been only a handful of instances, many of them in Texas. Some argue it's cruel and unusual punishment. But remember, these members can always join another service, such as HeavenNet or HellCom.

Of course, these punishments are null and void if you happen to be a celebrity. In that case, your fate will be a stiff dose of "community service." For instance, if you are a Hollywood action star who is caught while driving drunk, you'd be sent to a public school to tell the students that drunk driving is terrible, that you're very sorry, and that you won't be doing any drunk driving in your NEXT MOVIE, *Politics As Usual*, a delightful modern-day prince and pauper tale set in the White House! Coming soon to a theater near your school!

be a contingent that thinks it's fun to send flames, or "insults," as they're known off-line. We strongly discourage flaming. Granted, there are a handful of America Off-Line areas where the practice is allowed, even encouraged. (These include *Crossfire* on CNN, Don Rickles concerts and a New York City taxicab.) But on the whole, flaming is a big no-no.

Not only is it rude and inconsiderate, but off-line flame wars can be quite hurtful—even more hurtful than getting called a "luzer" or "pus-head." Take a look at some examples.

Flame: "Why don't you pry your atrophied brain out of your colon and shove it up your snot-packed, weevil-infested nose, where it belongs?"
Response flame: Punch to the sternum.

Flame: "You've got the IQ of a gherkin, the discernment of a cotton swab and a worldview simpler than that of a retarded four-year-old."
Response flame: Polo mallet in the forehead.

Flame: "Your nation is Satan's Lair, you are the Beastmaster, and I will continue to occupy this territory that is rightfully mine."
Response flame: Air strikes.

As we said, flame wars can get quite ugly, so avoid them at all costs. If you do become angry at someone, there are many, many options aside from face-to-face flames. You can take some deep breaths, go for a relaxing walk, or vow secretly to destroy your provoker's life. That's what I do. Why not call her husband and tell him about her nonexistent affair? Or phone her employer as a concerned representative of the methadone clinic? And so on. Easy!

Hackers

It's sad but true: The number of hackers on America Off-Line is on the rise. These unfriendly folks, known off-line as "robbers," access your Home Page with sophisticated hardware called Crowbars. Once inside, they steal your valuable files, especially ones with names like Strand of Pearls.

If you think you might have a hacker in your account, do NOT try to stop him yourself. As opposed to cyberspace, in the Real World hackers are not necessarily scrawny 14-year-old boys with 200 IQs, faces that look like pepperoni pizza, and a closetful of Nine Inch Nails T-shirts. Hackers instead carry switchblades and have bodies the size of Mt. McKinley. If you find one, call America Off-Line's special security division—the Police Department. (They're open 24 hours at 9-1-1.) They'll respond immediately, take down all the pertinent information, then go away and leave you alone for good.

Fortunately, things don't have to get that far. You can buy a whole range of hacker prevention software, including Locks, Alarm Systems and Doberman Pinschers.

Off-Line Addiction

We've got to admit, America Off-Line is terrific! With so many exciting features in Reality, it's no wonder we've got 250 million members. Still, it's important to remember that Reality is no substitute for cyberspace; both have their place in a balanced life.

Sadly, some of our members *don't* remember this. They start spending more and more time unplugged, as many as 16 or 17 hours a day! In short, they become addicted to Reality. This is very bad. It not

FREE
SPEECH

A s more and more people sign off, we're seeing an amazing revolution in the way humans communicate. But we're also seeing a whole wasp's nest of free speech issues buzzing to the fore. Here's our take on these challenging, brow-furrowing issues:

First of all, we believe that users of Reality should be granted the same freedom of speech that they enjoy in cyberspace. Our members should be able to express their opinions, no matter how smart or dumb.

Now that doesn't mean we're extremists. There should be limits to free speech in Reality, just as there are in cyberspace. For instance, when you're on-line, you shouldn't go into the Knitting Forum and type "THE SYSTEM IS CRASHING! THE SYSTEM IS CRASHING!" Similarly, when you're off-line, don't go into a crowded theater and shout "FIRE!" First of all, it would be a cliché. Second, everyone would leave, and miss the end of the movie, and have to rent it later, where it might be out, forcing them to rent a movie featuring a lesser Baldwin or an obscure Arquette, or even both.

A much stickier issue is pornography. Now we have to admit, our service has a LOT of pornography. Not only are there your run-of-the-mill magazines like *Playboy* and *Playgirl*, but there are also specialty publications where you can find, say, men expressing unnatural ardor for colonial furniture or women enjoying the company of bicuspids.

So what's the problem? Well, according to many parents, these naughty images are just too easily accessible by kids. For instance, a lot of pornography can be found in such convenient sites as Older Brother's Closet or Under Cousin Jimmy's Mattress. This makes some parents think there should be an off-line equivalent of the strict Communications Decency Act. But even if we blocked all off-line pornography, kids could still find a way to fire up the old modem and click to alt.nude.binaries.wilma.flintstone. In other words, stop blaming us!

only deprives you of important cyber-experiences, but it hurts those you care about, like your friends in the Monty Python newsgroup or the Fantasy Gaming chat room. As a service to you, here are some warning signs that indicate you may have a problem with off-line addiction.

1. You actually begin to get some color in your face.

2. You start getting the urge to spend more time with your "family." (You even know all their names!)

3. You have forgotten your password.

4. Your computer screen has toasters flying across it.

5. Your butt no longer conforms to the contours of a chair.

6. Your wrists stop aching.

7. You know which season it is.

8. You actually have to buy a new bar of Irish Spring.

9. You have ink stains on your fingers from off-line newspapers.

10. You've seen the latest Sean Connery movie in its entirety, not just a QuickTime clip on its Web site.

If any of these describe you, immediately fire up your modem!

THE OUTERNET

If you've been paying attention to the media lately, you've probably read about the Outernet. It seems every day there's another article adding to the hoopla, hollering and hype about this thing. The Outernet this, the Outernet that. Still, you may be confused, especially if you're not so smart. So let's take a closer look.

The first thing you should know is that no one owns the Outernet. No one controls it. Instead, it's a free-wheeling, global network of loosely connected services ("nations"). Sure, there's something called the UN that tries to ensure no single service entirely crashes the system with a nuclear bomb, but no one pays much attention.

The next thing you should know is that the Outernet is big. Huge! It spans everywhere from the North Pole to the South Pole and back again, incorporating the World Wide World. And talk about users! Although America Off-Line has a mighty respectable 250 million members, the Outernet has an astounding 5 billion. And climbing.

Why have so many people joined up? Well, the Outernet has got zillions of chat rooms, thousands of exciting sites, great graphics, and most importantly, it comes equipped with a feature called Gravity, which keeps people from drifting off.

> **CAUTION!** Before going any further, please understand that because America Off-Line does not control the Outernet, we cannot be responsible for its content. This is of special interest to parents, because there is much on the Outernet you don't want your kids exposed to: topless beaches, crazed terrorists, people who think Jerry Lewis is a genius....

Accessing the Outernet

Before venturing into this vast and exciting network, you'll need to get some new hardware and software:

A password. Or actually, as it's referred to on the Outernet, a pass*port*. The biggest difference between the two: the "passport" is generally accompanied by an image of you looking like you have to go to the bathroom. Still, the passport is just as important as the password. Do NOT give your passport to anyone, even if they promise to bring it right back.

Extra storage space. Or, in off-line jargon, a "fanny pack." This will not only store important files such as "maps" and "sunglasses," but it will immediately identify you as an America Off-Line member, giving you access to special deals such as $600 for an authentic local necklace made out of plastic.

A Web browser. These guides are similar to Yahoo! or Lycos, but they're called Frommer's and Michelin. They will guide you to the most interesting sites. Or at least what was most interesting when they were written four years ago, but which has since turned into a cream soda bottling plant.

An Outernet provider. America Off-Line has signed deals with several Outernet providers, including Delta, TWA, Qantas and Aer Lingus. Every day, these providers get better and better. But as with anything new and exciting, there are some kinks yet to be worked out. For instance, accessing the Outernet can still be a little slow. If you want to click to Europe.com, expect about eight hours of connect time, plus several additional hours of waiting at the gateway listening to a four-year-old speak at a decibel level appropriate to a Black Sabbath concert. Also, the omelettes suck.

The Outernet Chat Rooms

When you first step into an Outernet chat room, you may scratch your head. You'll hear phrases like "Bonjour" and "Cien pesos, por favor." Are these people using obscure acronyms you don't know? Not exactly. What's happening is they're speaking a totally different language.

Yes, just as the computer world has Java and HTML, the noncomputer world has French, Spanish and Cantonese. Granted, it wasn't always this way. At first, all off-line communication was done in binary code. "Grunt" meant good. "Groan" meant bad. But now that we're in the twentieth century, higher-level languages are used almost everywhere, with the exception of Jean-Claude Van Damme movies.

To survive in an Outernet chat room, you'll want to learn a few key phrases in the native language. Two that come in especially handy are "I'd like bottled water," and "No, I've never met David Hasselhoff."

CAUTION! It's disturbing but true: not everyone on the Outernet is a huge fan of America Off-Line. They think we're too successful, too "corporate." They'll cite some of our less-than-successful Outernet ventures, such as Vietnam and Eurodisney. They'll send you flames like "Yanqui go home!"

The best thing to do is give them a big old smiley and then run for your life. Everyone understands that. If that doesn't work, and you find yourself under house arrest, request to speak to one of our America Off-Line overseas customer service representatives, or "ambassadors."

A Short Tour of the World Wide World

When you're on the Outernet, you'll probably want to spend most of your time looking at the World Wide World, the section with the best graphics. Let's take a look at some sites!

http://www.paris.france.org
(Note: Experienced off-liners often drop all the notation and just say "Paris".)
Interactivity: Low. If you don't speak their language with a flawless accent, the hosts won't interact with you.
Graphic interface: Excellent. There are many lovely graphics, especially at the Louvre.

Speed: Slow. America Off-Line members can expect delays of two or three hours for, say, a croissant with ham.

http://www.rome.italy.org
Interactivity: High. Especially if you are a woman with a butt within pinching distance.
Graphic interface: Again, excellent. Although many of the features (i.e., "ruins") haven't been updated in a long time.
Speed: Medium. Under previous management, the trains ran on time. Now they don't.

http://www.acapulco.mexico.org
Interactivity: High. Many hormonal high school boys interact for as little as $20.
Graphic interface: Lots of graphic stuff goes on here. Nuff said.
Speed: Yes, and plenty of it. Other drugs too.

COOL SITES
http://www.reykjavíc.iceland.org
http://www.capehorn.chile.org
http://www.yakutsk.siberia.russia.org

HOT SITES
http://www.quito.ecuador.org
http://www.brisbane.australia.org
http://www.santodomingo.dominicanrepublic.org

SUCKIEST SITES
http://www.antartica.org
(This is considered a bit too kewl.)
http://www.cuba.org
(America Off-Line disagrees with this service's management style, and we encourage our members to stay away.)
http://www.chernobyl.plant.org
(This site has had some technical difficulties.)

THE FUTURE

America Off-Line is at the center of an exciting revolution. We're big, we're healthy, and we're perfectly poised to continue providing Reality into the new millennium and beyond.

Now some may say that's a bit too optimistic. Some say that Reality is just a fad, a blip on the screen, soon to go the way of Pong and Commodore 64s. We believe they're wrong. Reality is here to stay. Consider: The threat of nuclear war is waning. The Ebola virus has been contained. And there are no plans for a Gallagher sitcom. As you can see, it looks like the apocalypse is a few years off!

In the meantime, our service has lots going in its favor.

The America Off-Line Membership Base

Our membership continues to grow at an explosive rate, thanks to excellent word of mouth, strong promotions and a general lack of contraception. On average this year, we gained a new member once every 0.4 seconds, bringing us to a total of 250 million. Yes, 250 million: that's a 10,000 percent increase over our starting membership, about 200 years ago! (See "The Founding Members," page 98.)

In addition to the thousands of members who joined right out of the womb this year, many others switched over from other services, including Mexico Off-Line and GuatemalaServe. In fact, we got so many of these new recruits, some of our current members (User Name Pat Buchanan) suggest we refuse to accept any more. We think that's too severe. Sure, the ballooning membership base is causing some growing pains (e.g., high unemployment, urban riots, long lines at the Kwik-Mart), but we believe there is always room for more America Off-Line members!

One final bit of positive news: the member satisfaction—as measured by average retention rate—is higher than ever. Many of our members are staying with us well into their seventies and beyond, prompting us to upgrade such features as Home Care and *Matlock* reruns.

Expanding Business Opportunities

America Off-Line continues to stay ahead of the game in terms of research and development. Even as we speak, for instance, technicians at Paper Mate and Bic are working on better and more efficient Word Processors.

But perhaps just as excitingly, America Off-Line is pursuing an aggressive strategy of global expansion. Early on in our business's history, we actually tried to take over other services. We wanted them to use our operating system (Democracy 3.0, now available with

Newt Plus). Unfortunately, that strategy didn't work out very well, as evidenced by the failed hostile takeover of the Bay of Pigs.

Instead, we are now concentrating on forming joint business ventures with other services, allowing us to offer their features on our service. For instance, our members can buy BMWs from GermanyServe and Armani suits from ItalyNet. In return, we export *Baywatch*. It's all part of the exciting interconnectedness of the Outernet!

THE FOUNDING
MEMBERS

How did America Off-Line get started? Back in the 1700s, a mangy band of venture capitalists got fed up with paying the unreasonable user fees charged by Brit.com and decided to sign off. In 1776, they formed their own service, dedicated to, among other things, providing a wide range of Religious Forums.

Under the visionary management of our first CEO (User Name George Washington), we were able to ratchet up the off-line security system and install a relatively fair user fee schedule. Since Washington, America Off-line has gone through a few dozen CEOs, all of whom have helped expand America Off-Line's services and range. User Name Thomas Jefferson established dozens of local access numbers west of Louisiana. User Name Abraham Lincoln oversaw a particularly unpleasant management disagreement, after which he issued a new class of shares. And under User Name Woodrow Wilson, America Off-Line extended voting privileges to Class F shareholders.

The current CEO has to deal with an even vaster domain than previous ones, including making sure that motel maid in Tucson gets her hush money.

An Off-Line Techno-History

Perhaps the strongest proof that Reality isn't a fad comes from the impressive history of off-line technological advancements, on both our service and others. Here's a look at some of the highlights:

300 B.C.: An early version of the Word Processor ("pencil") is fashioned out of reeds.

105 A.D.: A member named Ts'ai Lun makes the first true "pages" out of mulberry fish nets and hemp.

1454: Johannes Gutenberg becomes the Steve Jobs of his day by making data available to the masses.

1477: Louis XI of France.Net sets up one of the first nonelectronic Mail systems—the Royal Postal Service—using 230 mounted couriers.

1564: A graphite mine (think of it as "Graphite Valley") is discovered in Brit.com, enabling widespread manufacture of the Word Processor.

1719: A scientist gets the idea to use trees (see "Log" in "Glossary," page 115) for making "pages" after watching wasps make their nests.

1806: It becomes a whole lot easier to back up your files. User Name Ralph Wedgewood invents carbon paper.

1816: Some early advocates of off-line life (called Luddites) destroy proto-computers.

1837: A politician in Brit.com introduces huge

reforms to nonelectronic mail, including prepaid stamps.

1867: A company called Remington invents a new type of Word Processor, the Typewriter.

1875: A global association called the Universal Postal Union makes mail to the Outernet feasible.

1884: America Off-Line's own L. E. Waterman improves on the Word Processor with his new Fountain Pen.

1938: Another America Off-Line member, Chester Carlson, makes backing up files even more simple with his Xerox machine.

1939: Yet another improvement on the Word Processor. Two brothers named Biro manufacture the first workable Ballpoint Pens.

![HELP!]

Here at America Off-Line, we've tried to make Reality as user-friendly as possible. Still, it's a brave new world, and there's no doubt it can get a little confusing. Inevitably, questions will come up, heads will be scratched, brows will be furrowed, chairs will be thrown against walls. Well, don't worry. America Off-Line has a comprehensive Customer Support system. Our specialists are ready to assist you with any and all questions. They come in many stripes.

Live Technical Support

If you're having trouble working America Off-Line, the first thing you should do is try our 24-hour Customer Information Line. Someone is standing by right now! Simply pick up the telephone, dial 4-1-1, and ask away. How do I get my "pencil" to write in italics? What's the best site for finding Romance? If they sound bewildered, or even a bit irritated, remind them that they are called "Information," and this is the information you want.

The Bulletin Boards

If you don't need help right away, why not try the extensive Bulletin Board system? You're probably familiar with these from cyberspace. Well, it's the same idea, except ours are made of cork and use pointy little fellows called pushpins. Bulletin boards are the perfect place to post requests such as "Anyone going to Boston?—I need a ride" or "Looking for a sunny one-bedroom with a view." Expect a response within a week. But be careful. On America Off-Line, Bulletin Boards are often located in sites like the Office and Grocery Store, which means you should refrain from questions like "Does anyone know whether it's legal to have sex with a cow if the cow gives its consent?" Though acceptable on many cyber-boards, this would draw strange looks from off-line passersby.

Members Helping Members

Your fellow America Off-Line members aren't merely potential "friends"—they're potential experts. No doubt, they've picked up some helpful knowledge in their travels through Reality. In fact, there's an expert right next door: He's called your "neighbor"! Simply knock on his door and ask away. Where's the nearest Post Office? How do you get to Maple Street? When can you expect his goddamn dog to stop eating the yams in your garden? Has he ever seen your powerful Smith and Wesson shotgun?

Technical Support: Extreme Cases

Sometimes our members experience more complex technical problems. Sometimes their entire system of Reality goes on the fritz. In this case, they have several options, the first being the Self-Help Manuals. These "books," all easily downloadable at the Local Bookstore, offer you tips on rebooting your system yourself. According to them, the major problem is one of perception. Although you may think your system is broken, it really isn't! Off-line, this is called "low self-esteem."

If these don't seem to be working, you might want to try another self-help manual called the Bible. You've heard of the *PC Bible*. Well, this is just the Bible, plain and simple. The Bible has been around a long time and was written by someone named God, who is sort of like Bill Gates, only less wealthy. Well, technically God didn't actually write the Bible. He didn't pick up the Word Processor or anything. Instead, God came up with all the ideas, but like Gates, he had a ghostwriter, probably a free-

HELP!

If all else fails, and you're really in dire need of assistance, there's yet another option. You can simply start screaming "HELP! HELP!" Unfortunately, this doesn't work very well in major metropolitan areas, as everyone around you will suddenly start studying the interesting cement patterns in the sidewalk.

lance stringer for the *Bethlehem Star-Tribune* or something. We'll never know, because he or she isn't named, not even in the acknowledgments.

In any case, God is pretty knowledgeable about Reality systems, and provides several important suggestions for making sure yours stays intact. If you don't have time to read the whole manual, simply turn to the 10 dos and don'ts (aka "Commandments"). In these, God says "Thou shalt not download nude GIFs of thy neighbor's wife," "Thou shalt not pirate software," etc. Or something like that, anyway.

But, you say, you've tried the Bible and other Self-Help Manuals, and you're still experiencing problems. In this case, you might want to contact a customer specialist called the "psychiatrist." Since "psychiatrists" cost about as much as a majority stake in Netscape, you should be really sure you need one, absolutely certain your system has crashed. For instance:

Are you having trouble getting out of bed in the morning?

Do you think that former president Millard Fillmore is trying to get an important message to you?

Do you sleep in an oxygen chamber and own all the rights to Beatles songs?

If you answered "yes" to any of the above, you're indeed ready for this service. What do these psychiatrists do? Think of them as hackers of the mind, technicians so adept they are licensed by the state. Their bag of tricks includes interrogation, mind-altering substances and endless questions about sex. The process takes a little while—say, 17 years or so—but at least you get to read *Architectural Digest*s from 1983 in the waiting room.

More Support

As if that's not enough! Here's a look at other types of America Off-Line customer support: Crutches, canes, walkers, orthopedic shoes, Wonderbras.

Q: *What happens if I forget my User Name?*
A: You'd be surprised how rarely this happens on America Off-Line, unless you happen to be a character in a soap opera. Try looking in your wallet—you'll see your User Name printed on your "driver's license."

Q: *I'm thinking of terminating my America Off-Line account. Whom do I call?*
A: Take a couple minutes to call our staff members who deal with just this situation. They can be reached at the Suicide Hotline. Tell them your complaints with our service ("My husband is cheating on me, my kids hate me, and I'm bankrupt") and they'll provide advice over the phone ("Have you tried a McDonald's Happy Meal?"). If you do decide that you still want to terminate your membership, try not to do it all over the expensive Oriental rug. That doesn't help anybody.

FREQUENTLY ASKED QUESTIONS

What's the secret to America Off-Line's success? We've got a few of them. Two hundred and fifty million of them, to be exact. That's right. It's YOU, the members, who are responsible! That's why we feel very strongly about personally responding to each and every letter that we get. Here's a sample of some FAQs:

> Dear America Off-Line,
> I have a personal Home Page on the
> World Wide Web. Is there something
> similar I can do in Reality?
> Maxine Tyler
> Philadelphia, Pennsylvania

Dear Maxine,
As a matter of fact, you *can* carve out your own little corner of Reality, your own little domain. It's called, quite simply, a Home. But you should know that there are some key differences between Homes and Home Pages. Here's a look:

Hits

On your Home Page, the more visitors the better. Dozens, hundreds, thousands—come on in, day or night! Not so for your Home. At your Home, you want only a small trickle of hits per month, maybe 10 or 15. And each visitor should stay longer than the on-line average of 30 seconds. More like three hours. A visitor who surfs from Home to Home every half minute is considered very rude, or else a Jehovah's Witness.

Designing a Home

If you want to set up your own Home, you'll need some basic hardware: hammer, nails, two-by-fours, etc. But except for our Amish members, very few of our customers build their own Homes off-line. Instead, you should hire a professional designer (called an "architect"), some professional programmers ("construction workers"), and then before you know it (i.e., before the sun turns into a black hole), you've got a cute little Home.

Personal Data

Just as with Home Pages on the Web, off-line Homes have a place where you can store all sorts of personal data. This is called a "diary." Here you can enter anything you want—from a long list of your favorite movies, to some boys you had crushes on in sixth grade, to an amusing anecdote about your orthodontist's bad breath. What's really interesting about the diary, though, is that, except in rare cases, NOBODY READS IT BUT YOU!! This is much more efficient. This way, other members don't waste half an hour clicking through menu after menu on your Home Page, only to find an index of your bas mitzvah presents.

Similarly, visitors should NOT be treated to your résumé. The résumé should be kept well hidden in a desk drawer, to be taken out only when "mailing" job "applications."

Links

In the off-line world, "links" are used in fencing material, which actually keeps Homes apart, rather than leading you from one to the next. Ironic, yes?

```
Dear America Off-Line,
You know those text files (or "books")
in the Library of Congress? Why don't
you translate them all into Klingon?
                        Steve Jenkins
                    Bethesda, Maryland
```

Dear Steve,

Thanks for the suggestion! At one point, we thought about doing just that. The problem is, strange as it may sound, in the off-line world, the interest level in *Star Trek* is not as high as you might think.

Want proof? Try this test. Ask some random America Off-Line members what they think of Spock, and watch them start yammering about breast-feeding and child care and other un-Vulcan-like stuff.

As much as we may think they're crazy to miss out on Trek, you have to understand this: America Off-Line is just so packed with other options—including the activity known as "having a life"—that many members just don't have time to soak up all the genius of Commander Roddenberry.

So instead, we at America Off-Line decided to translate many of the books into other, non-Klingon languages. Like French and Chinese (see "The Outernet," page 91). Why not "boldly go" and learn these fascinating tongues?

Dear America Off-Line,
Why aren't there more female members on
America Off-Line? We need more chicks!

Dave Floria
Buffalo, New York

Dear Dave,
Actually, unlike some on-line services, America Off-Line does have a large number of female customers. In fact, of our 250 million members, slightly more than half are women!

Perhaps the problem you're encountering is that you are spending time at the wrong America Off-Line sites. That often happens to those who have just signed off for the first time. Let me give you some hints: Going to your friend's house to play Dungeons and Dragons isn't the best way to meet women. *Mystery Science Theater 3000* conventions also have a disproportionate number of guys.

Why not try the Theater site? Or the Museum?

Dear America Off-Line,
The Real World is so loud! I can hardly
hear myself think!! Can you please tell
me how to turn down the volume?

Kimberly Picon
San Diego, California

Dear Kimberly,
Good point. America Off-Line has some wonderful sound effects. You can hear a droplet (access a sink), a quack (access a duck pond), a wind chime (access a hippie's house), and even a wild eep (access a wild eep watering hole). But you're right. Sometimes things get just a little too loud.

So that's why we've built in a volume control. To activate it, place your hands over your ears. Now hold them there. Hope that helps!

Dear America Off-Line,
What is your hot list?

Mariah Stoddard
Memphis, Tennessee

Dear Mariah,
Thanks for asking. Here's my hot list, or as we say off-line, "a few of my favorite things":
1. Raindrops on roses
2. Whiskers on kittens
3. Bright copper kettles
4. Warm woolen mittens
5. Brown paper packages tied up with string
6. Girls in white dresses with blue satin sashes
7. Snowflakes that stay on my nose and eyelashes
8. Latex bikini briefs for men

Dear America Off-Line,
In cyberspace, Courtney Love is
notorious for her abrasive postings.
Is there anyone off-line who is
similarly abrasive?

Jessica Watts
Phoenix, Arizona

Dear Jessica,
Yes. Her name is, uh, Courtney Love.

Dear America Off-Line,
What's a "dork"?

Harold Wright
Baltimore, Maryland

Dear Harold,
A "dork" is someone who has just signed off. It's the equivalent of the word newbie, and the overtones are just as hostile. Sadly, some veterans of America Off-Line selfishly want to keep "dorks" out, figuring they'll clog everything and make parking even harder than it is now. If you've just signed off for the first time, Reality-heads may try to confuse you. They'll throw around technical jargon like "nature" and "trees" and "hiking." Don't be afraid to ask what these are. Although you may initially get beaten up, before long, you'll be able to taunt newcomers yourself.

Dear America Off-Line,
I heard that children can learn how to build bombs off-line. Is this true?

Casey Wiggums
Portland, Maine

Dear Casey,
No doubt, with so much information off-line, there's the risk that your child might be exposed to something terrible like this. Still, it's no reason to keep kids from the wonderful world of Reality! You just have to keep your eye on them. For instance, if you hear your child asking the department store Santa for "a pony, a sweater and four quarts of nitroglycerine," you might want to have a talk with her.

```
Dear America Off-Line,
I recently started a romantic attach-
ment to an America Off-Line User named
Bill, whom I met at the Laundromat. I
haven't told my cybermate SiliPutty. Am
I cheating on him?
                        Hallie Scotchman
                   Indianapolis, Indiana
```

Dear Hallie,

Well, we're not exactly http://www.annlanders.com. But we can say this: Studies show that it *is* possible to form real emotional attachments in your off-line relationships. In other words, there's probably a reason you're not telling SiliPutty. Maybe you feel there's a real chance that you and Bill have a future together, and not just in Reality, but in cyberspace too. Perhaps it's time you started trading e-mails with Bill to see if you can form a lasting relationship. Only then will you know.

```
Dear America Off-Line,
What's the best way to get around your
service?
                        Janice Moorehead
                  Santa Cruz, California
```

Dear Janice,

As you may have noticed, pointing-and-clicking is pretty uncommon out there in Reality. So how do you get from one site to another? Well, you can use those things located under your desk, called "legs," and try to "walk." Or you can use the Noninfo Highway, that much-ballyhooed system devised by Al Gore's father. Here's a look:

Hardware

Instead of a modem, you'll need a Car, which comes in both external (aka Convertible) and internal (aka "everything else") varieties.

Speed

No matter whether you have a high-speed Car (Maserati) or a low-speed Car (a 1974 Plymouth Valiant), the Noninfo Highway only supports 65 bauds (aka "miles per hour"). If you need to go faster, move to GermanyServe or get a woman in labor to sit in the passenger seat.

No-nos

The Noninfo Highway is no place for child pornography. Wait until you get home to read it. Otherwise, it might distract you from driving.

GLOSSARY

All this technical jargon in the Real World—it's enough to send you hightailing it back to the warm cocoon of cyberspace. Well, buck up, buster! This easy-to-understand glossary should clear everything up.

Operating Terms

Agent
A life form that searches the off-line world for "deals," "foreign rights," and "Evian water."

Applications
What you have to fill out after you get fired from your job for surfing the Web all day. Killer App: One with the words "senior vice president" on it.

C+
A decent grade in the America Off-Line Educational Forums—but nothing that would get you into MIT.

Client
Someone you have to pretend to lose to in tennis, especially when you're the "server."

Dingbats
People of low intelligence. See Yahoo.

Driver

A member who takes you from one site to another. However, unless your company just did an IPO, you can't afford a driver.

Error

When a ball sneaks through a first baseman's mitt.
Also, Fatal Error
When that ball happens to be in the sixth game of the Mets/Red Sox World Series.

Finder

Person who gains ownership, as in "finders, keepers."

Icon

An image or a picture—but instead of a garbage can or a floppy disk, it's usually Jesus Christ or the Virgin Mary. And instead of dragging it, you worship it.

Joystick

Something used in noncybersex.

Log (verb)

To use PowerTools to erase a forest. "Log on" means to keep on logging.

Lotus

A yellow, purple or white flower. Legend has it that the plant induces a drowsy state, much like filling out a spreadsheet on Lotus 1-2-3.

Mud

A multi-user game. The full name of the game is Rolling Around in the Mud, and it's played by two or more younger users who want to get all messy and torment their parents. Can also be played by bikini-clad women in front of a bunch of drooling, beer-drinking Neanderthals.

Myst (off-line, spelled Mist)
A type of weather. Mist can be just as time-consuming as the CD-ROM, especially if you're at an airport, waiting for takeoff.

Net
A system where you might find fish, butterflies or fallen acrobats, but rarely essays about how Dilbert is God.

PC
In Reality, this stands for "politically correct," not "personal computer." People who are PC go out of their way not to offend others. For instance, they might use a phrase like "monitor of color."

PDA
Another confusing acronym that stands for "public display of affection," not "personal digital assistant." It refers to members who forgot to go to a Private Room.

Sleep mode
What people go into in Reality between the hours of midnight and 8:00 a.m. when you're busy posting important messages on the alt.fan.douglas-adams newsgroup. To get a person out of Sleep mode, press any "key" (or the whole "key chain") into their forehead.

Surf
To ride the network of water known as the Ocean using boards, not bauds.

Wang
See Joystick.

Window
An off-screen frame that displays the Outdoors site. On America Off-Line, you can open several "windows" at once. In fact, you can open as many as you want, as long as it's not 20 degrees below zero.

Warning: "Windows" sometimes let in "bugs."

Wired
Extremely awake. The opposite of Sleep mode. Can result when you drink too much Java (see below).

Yahoo
A member who spends a lot of time reading the Jeff Foxworthy home page.

Power Sources

Off-line, the word "feed" refers to more than a data stream. It also refers to the act of stuffing one's face to gain energy. Here are just a few of the available options.

Apple
An inexpensive, user-friendly fruit. The "apple" has a long off-line history. When User Name Eve ate an "apple," she was kicked out of the Garden of Eden, just like Steve Jobs was kicked out of the Apple management committee. Isaac Newton had an "apple" drop on his head, which led to the invention of electronic Filofaxes.

Hot Links
A type of food also known as a "sausage." It's created by a program similar to StuffIt.

Java
A beverage that goes well with Hot Links. Often used as an accelerator.

Spam
A food substance from Hormel made up of animal parts (see "Spamming," page 39). It's presumably

named after spamming, because it clogs your system. In this case, the artery system.

Organic Intelligence

In the off-line world, there is a class of beings that isn't quite human, but not quite electronic either. These are called "animals," and here's a look at some of them.

Gopher
This searches the Outernet for files such as "nuts and berries."

MOO
The sound emitted by an animal called "the cow." The MOO doesn't make for a really interesting multi-user game, unless you happen to be a couple of five-year-olds singing "Old McDonald Had a Farm."

Mouse
This little guy—yes, about the same size as your computer mouse—has many functions. You can "point" at the mouse, often accompanied by the vocal expression "Eeeeek!" You can "click" the mouse on the head with a broom or a tennis racket. And then you can "drag" the mouse outside of your house.

RAM
An animal that, unlike its computer cousin, isn't particularly known for its memory. For that, you'll have to look at an even bigger creature called an "elephant."

TurboMouse
Speedy Gonzales.

A.J. Jacobs is a staff writer for "Entertainment Weekly" magazine, and author of "The Two Kings" (Bantam, 1994), a look at the eerie similarities between Jesus and Elvis. His work has also appeared in "The New York Observer," "The Utne Reader," and "Glamour." He's been intrigued by Reality for several years now.

This document was composed in Deadline, a font designed by author A. J. Jacobs.

UPGRADE YOUR HUMOR SOFTWARE

If you enjoyed *America Off-Line*, you might enjoy downloading some other recent humor files (known to your local retailer as "books," or to your more literary retailer as "non-books") from Cader Books.

D o you know which screen diva was arrested for castrating a donkey? Or which rock idol was caught peeing on the Alamo? *Famous Mugs* has the answers, in words and actual booking photos, for over 200 celebrities.

ISBN: 0-8362-1503-6
$7.95

H ere are dozens of delicious high-fat recipes secretly known to be favored by the President—straight from the mouth of the bestselling Anonymous. A veritable "primary calories," each chapter brims over with honest American cooking, from French Fried Nation and Slick Sneakin' Food to Willie Con Queso.

ISBN: 0-8362-1497-8
$8.95

S *trange Days #1* (by the editors of the British cult classic magazine *Fortean Times*) collects real-life "X-Files" subjects from around the globe, from UFOs and poltergeists to natural wonders, zany coincidences, and odd incidents—like the chef who was stabbed through the heart with uncooked spaghetti strands.

ISBN: 0-8362-1499-4
$9.95

T *hat's Funny!* gathers together all of your favorite comedians—from Ellen, Seinfeld, and Roseanne to Tim Allen, Brett Butler, Jeff Foxworthy, and more—and all their favorite lines in one great comedy club.

ISBN: 0-8362-1502-8
$9.95

Available now from your local retailer.